The European Football Championships

By

Liam McCann

About the author

Liam McCann was born in Guildford, England, in 1973. He attended Hurstpierpoint College and Staffordshire University, gaining a Bachelor of Arts degree in Sports Physiology and Psychology. Growing up, he excelled on the sports field, becoming county champion in three of the athletics field events and swimming to a national standard. He went on to win a British University medal in 1993. Liam then formed a rock band that toured Europe. The group's highlight came in 2001 when they played to five thousand people. In 2003 he turned his hand to writing non-fiction sports and reference books. He has since had 14 published and is currently working on an action / thriller series featuring hero Ed Sampson.

By Liam McCann

When the Messenger meets the King
In the Lap of the Gods
The Devil's Breath
Rolling Thunder
The Battle of Boxhill

Non-fiction

The Olympics Facts, Figures & Fun
Rugby Facts, Figures & Fun
Cricket Facts, Figures & Fun
The Sledger's Handbook
Born to Dribble
The Revised & Expanded Sledger's Handbook
The European Football Championships
UFOs: Fact or Fiction?
Little Book of Survival
Little Book of the Universe
Little Book of Liners
Little Book of HMS Ark Royal

With Sue Todd

Little Book of the Royal Air Force, Red Arrows Edition

With Andrew O'Brien

The World's Greatest Sporting Rivalries

With Hans Potter

The Little English Boy

Introduction

A brief history of the European Football Championships

Held every four years, the European Championships represent the pinnacle of international football in Europe. It is arguably more difficult to win the tournament than the World Cup because the continent is traditionally strong in the sport and the overall quality of the opposition is better. (There are no so-called minnows like New Zealand or any of the Caribbean islands.) Instead, having qualified, which is difficult enough, your team is likely to come up against the cream of European football in the shape of France, Germany, England, Italy and current world champions, Spain. However, throughout the tournament's rich history, some surprise winners have emerged, such as Denmark in 1992 and Greece in 2004.

French football administrator Henri Delaunay, who had previously played for Paris side Étoile des Deux Lacs before taking up refereeing, proposed a continental football championship in 1927. His initial suggestion was ignored so he teamed up with Jules Rimet and became one of the architects of the first World Cup in 1930. He campaigned vigorously for a European tournament to be held in the even years between World Cups but it wasn't until the 1950s that the national federations began to take his idea seriously. He became UEFA's first General Secretary when the federation was formed in 1954 but he died the following year and just missed seeing his vision become a reality. The championship trophy is still named after him, however. The growing popularity of European club football undoubtedly swayed the undecided but it would be another five years before the first team tournament was held, the inaugural UEFA European Nations Cup, in

7

France in 1960.

The competition was almost cancelled at the last minute because several national football associations reneged on the deal and there were too few teams to compete, but seventeen sides eventually signed up to the tournament (although Italy, West Germany, England, Ireland, Scotland and Wales were not among them). The Spanish were forced to withdraw after General Franco refused to allow the team to go to Moscow for a quarter-final against the Soviet Union.

The original format was vastly different from today's well-organised and meticulously planned event. Qualifying was staged over two years with teams playing each other home and away in knockout games. Four teams eventually emerged and went on to a semi-final spot. The host nation was only chosen after qualifying, so they had to come from one of the four semi-finalists.

Initial fears about how popular the tournament would be were dispelled when more than a hundred thousand people watched the USSR beat Hungary 3-1 in the first qualifying match in Moscow. France, Czechoslovakia and Yugoslavia joined the Soviet Union in the semi-finals and the French were then chosen as hosts for the last phase. Led by their outstanding goalkeeper, Lev Yashin, the Soviet Union comfortably beat the Czechs (3-0) in the first semi-final in Marseille. Then Yugoslavia came from behind twice to beat the hosts in a nine-goal thriller (5-4). Yugoslavia's Galić opened the scoring in the final, but Metreveli equalised five minutes later. The game was still level after ninety minutes so it went to extra time. With seven minutes left on the clock a header from Viktor Ponedelnik sealed the win for the Soviet Union at the Parc des Princes in front of eighteen thousand fans.

Four years later, twenty-nine teams entered the qualification round. This time it was Greece's turn to withdraw because they were pitted against Albania, a country with which they were at war. After another convoluted qualifying process, Denmark, Hungary, Spain (chosen as hosts), and the Soviet Union all made it to the final stages. The USSR dispatched the Danes 3-0 in Barcelona and Spain set up a showdown with them (Franco, remember, had refused to allow the Spanish side to travel to the USSR during the first tournament) after defeating Hungary 2-1 in Madrid. In stifling heat at the Santiago Bernabéu, Spain won 2-1 after a late Marcelino goal gave them their first major trophy in front of eighty thousand people.

The initial knockout stages in 1968 were replaced by qualification groups and the cup was renamed the European Championship. Thirty-one teams entered the competition but only four made it to the last stage in Italy. The Soviet Union were unlucky not to make a third consecutive final. Their match against the hosts was still 0-0 after extra time, but, as there were no penalty shootouts in those days, the game was decided by the toss of a coin, which Italy won. In the second semi-final England's world champions were beaten by 1-0 Yugoslavia. The final in the Olympic stadium in Rome ended 1-1, but Italy beat Yugoslavia 2-0 in the replay at the same venue two days later in front of fifty-five thousand people.

Rome's superb Stadio Olimpico

Qualifying for the 1972 finals in Belgium took place during 1970 and 1971, with only four teams from an initial thirty-two making it to the final stages. The hosts were joined by Hungary, the Soviet Union and West

The victorious Italians at Euro '68
10 Rls POSTAGE AJMAN ١٠ ریال برید حجمالن

Germany. The incomparable Gerd Müller scored both goals to give a classy West German side victory over Belgium in the first semi-final, while the Soviet Union beat Hungary 1-0 in the second match to reach the final for the third time. Gerd Müller scored another two in a 3-0 West German victory over the USSR in the final at the ill-fated Heysel Stadium in Brussels in front of forty-four thousand. This victory ushered in a period of dominance for the Germans and they would go on to win the 1974 World Cup on home soil.

The final European Championship under these rules was held in Yugoslavia in 1976. Thirty-two teams were again whittled down to the final four: hosts Yugoslavia, West Germany, the Netherlands and Czechoslovakia. West Germany again made it to the final (at the expense of Yugoslavia) to meet underdogs Czechoslovakia who had beaten the Netherlands 3-1. The final finished 2-2 and a penalty shootout was needed to separate the teams. West German Uli Hoeneß missed his spot-kick but the Czechs slotted their five, including an outrageous chip by Antonín Panenka, to lift the trophy in front of thirty-one thousand fans in Belgrade.

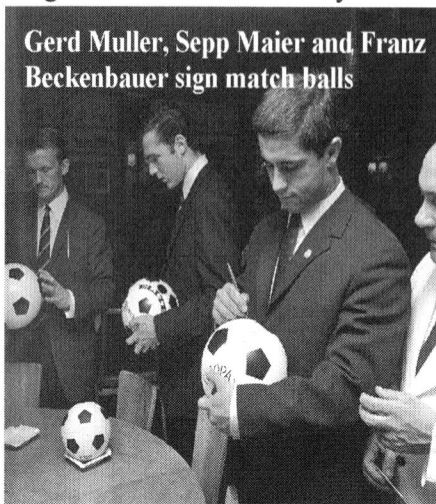

Gerd Muller, Sepp Maier and Franz Beckenbauer sign match balls

The competition was given a major overhaul before Euro '80 in Italy but the tournament will be remembered for a number of poor defensively oriented matches and several outbreaks of hooliganism, most notably during the England – Belgium fixture when police were forced to use teargas to crush rioting fans. The hosts were chosen before the event and qualified automatically, and seven more teams joined them after the qualifying rounds: Belgium, Czechoslovakia, England, Greece, the Netherlands, Spain and West Germany. These eight were split into two groups, with the winners from each progressing directly into the final (the two runners-up played a third place match). Spectator numbers were also down with most only turning out for matches involving the hosts. The Belgians provided most of the excitement and made it to the final against a talented young German side, although they

Antonin Panenka's delicate chip won the 1976 tournament.

eventually lost 2-1 in Rome's Olympic stadium in front of forty-eight thousand people.

The French hosted a successful Euro '84 tournament that saw a number of changes to the format. This time group winners and runners-up would meet in a pair of semi-finals, with the two winners going onto the final. The third place match, which was often dull as it was being played by demoralised teams and had nothing riding on the result, was dropped from the program. Seven state-of-the-art stadiums, good crowds and entertaining games brought the championships into the modern era. An inspired Michel Platini lit up the event with two hat-tricks and goals in every game as France brushed everyone else aside, including title contenders Belgium (5-0). They also beat Denmark (1-0) and then saw off Yugoslavia (3-2) to set up a tie against the exciting Portuguese.

The semi-final has been voted one of the greatest international matches of all time. France took an early lead but Portugal equalised late on and sent the game into extra time. Then Rui Jordão scored his second to give Portugal the lead but Jean-François Domergue soon fired home his second. The match looked to be heading for penalties until Platini's last-minute winner saw them through to a final against old rivals Spain. The final will be remembered for a horrible blunder by Spanish goalkeeper Luis Arconada, in which he let a Platini free-kick squirm under his body. Despite rallying against the ten-man French, the Spanish could not find the net and they eventually lost 2-0.

Having won only one match in the build-up to the Euro '88 Championships in West Germany, France finished behind East Germany and the USSR in their group, so the defending champions failed to qualify for the tournament. There were several protests at England's inclusion in the final eight (they joined the hosts, Denmark, Italy, the Netherlands, Republic of Ireland, Spain and the Soviet Union) because of the Heysel Stadium disaster, but they were eventually allowed to compete. The hosts had a strong team (with

Juventus's Michel Platini with the Ballon d'Or in 1985

Jürgen Klinsmann, Jürgen Kohler, Lothar Matthäus, Pierre Littbarski, and Thomas Berthold) and were favourites to win on home soil. England were also expected to do well after an excellent qualification campaign and with a team including Glenn Hoddle, Bryan Robson, Chris Waddle, John Barnes, Peter Beardsley and Gary Lineker. However, English confidence was misplaced and they were knocked out after three defeats, including losing 1-0 to the Republic of Ireland, conceding a hat-trick to Marco van Basten, and

Marco van Basten hits his famous volley at Euro '88

then being dumped out of the tournament 3-1 by the Soviet Union. Italy also had an excellent young side including Paolo Maldini, Riccardo Ferri, Gianluca Vialli and Roberto Mancini, and they went through to the semi-finals with hosts West Germany. In Group B, the USSR and the Netherlands also progressed to the semi-finals. The Netherlands beat the hosts in the first semi, a late Van Basten strike sealing victory. The Soviet Union, with the core of its team built around the excellent Dynamo Kiev side, joined them after a comfortable 2-0 victory over Italy in Stuttgart. The Soviet Union couldn't cope with the excellent Dutch side of Ruud Gullit, Marco van Basten, Frank Rijkaard, Ronald Koeman, Gerald Vanenburg and veteran Arnold Mühren, and they eventually lost 2-0 in Munich's Olympic stadium in front of a seventy-two-thousand-strong crowd. Gullit's bullet header in the first half and Van Basten's wonderful dipping volley just after the break are two of football's most enduring images. Strangely, no one was sent off during the tournament, none of the matches went to penalties and there was at least one goal in every game.

Yugoslavia had descended into a bloody civil war and their fabulously talented team was withdrawn from Euro '92 in Sweden. United Nations sanctions were imposed and their place was handed to the runners-up in their qualification group, Denmark. The Soviet Union was also breaking up and five of the states did not contribute any players to the new CIS squad. Indeed, it was a time of social and political change across the continent, and a reunified Germany competed under one flag for the first time in thirty years. Germany, Sweden, England (after a superb performance at the Italia '90 World

Cup) and the Netherlands were considered the teams to beat, yet England again failed to live up to expectations and finished bottom of their group without a win. With the French also failing to make it through, Group A was topped by the hosts and the Danes. Scotland and the CIS did predictably poorly in Group B and the Germans and another strong Dutch side went through to the semi-finals. Germany saw off the hosts (3-2) after an excellent match in Solna, and Denmark, recalled from their holidays at the last minute, made it to the final after a battling performance against the Netherlands finished 2-2. The exceptional Danish goalkeeper, Peter Schmeichel, then saved Van Basten's penalty to see them through to a final against the Germans in Gothenburg. Schmeichel was called upon again and delivered an outstanding goalkeeping display to thwart wave after wave of German attacks. At the other end, John Jensen scored a rare goal after eighteen minutes and a classic strike from Kim Vilfort in the closing stages won a game watched by thirty-eight thousand.

Peter Schmeichel celebrates Denmark's unlikely win at Euro '92

Hosts England were, yet again, tipped to do well at Euro '96, and this time they delivered (the tournament had been expanded to sixteen teams divided into four groups of four). England recovered from a disappointing 1-1 draw with Switzerland to lift themselves for a match against their oldest international rivals, Scotland. Paul Gascoigne then scored one of the goals of the tournament, flicking the ball over defender Colin Hendry and volleying past Andy Goram to seal a 2-0 victory. They then put past conservatism behind them with a devastating attacking display against the much-fancied Netherlands, trouncing them 4-1. The single Dutch goal proved vital because it sent the Scots home on goal difference and the Netherlands sneaked through to the next round. Pre-tournament favourites Italy were plagued by infighting and couldn't make it past the group stages, and the Germans and the Czech Republic qualified for the quarter-finals instead. A strong French side was building towards their own World Cup and they qualified for the tournament's knockout stages along with Spain from Group B. Portugal and Croatia made it through from Group D.

Scotland take on Holland at Euro '96

England then beat an unlucky Spanish side (they had two goals wrongly disallowed that might have handed them victory) on penalties, with goalkeeper David Seaman on sparkling form, to set up a repeat of the 1990 World Cup semi-final against a German side that had eased past Croatia (2-1) at Old Trafford in Manchester. The Czech Republic squeezed past Portugal to face the French, who had put the underperforming Dutch out on penalties. The first semi-final between England and Germany was tense. Alan Shearer headed England into an early lead but Stefan Kuntz pulled one back ten minutes later. England had a number of chances to win it – Darren Anderton hit the post and Paul Gascoigne failed to score with the goal at his mercy – and the game went to extra time. The half hour couldn't separate them and, once again, a match between the two went to penalties. And, once again, England were

Alan Shearer wheels away after scoring the opener against Germany in the semi-final of Euro '96 at Wembley Stadium

knocked out, going down 6-5 after Gareth Southgate's spot-kick was saved. The Czech Republic also progressed to the final after rather drab victories over Portugal and France in the knockout stages. In a Wembley final watched by more than seventy thousand people, Patrick Berger put the underdog Czechs in front from the penalty spot, but Olivier Bierhoff levelled the match fifteen minutes later. It was still tied at 1-1 after ninety minutes so the game went to extra time. Germany scored the first Golden Goal in a major final to take the trophy after Czech 'keeper Petr Kouba failed to save a miss-hit shot by Oliver Bierhoff. It was their record third win in the competition.

Forty-nine teams from nine qualifying groups were finally whittled down to the sixteen who would compete for the trophy during Euro 2000, which was co-hosted by Belgium and the Netherlands. Norway and Slovenia made it to the tournament proper for the first time. Portugal and Romania surprised England and Germany by topping Group A. It had been another tournament to forget for a much-fancied England side. They led Portugal 2-0 before rolling over meekly and going down 3-2, but they fought back to beat Germany 1-0. A draw against Romania would have been good enough to see them through but a last-minute penalty gave Romania victory. Italy won all three of their Group B matches, dragging Turkey through to the next round in second place. Spain and Yugoslavia saw off the challenge from both debutants to top Group C, and strong sides from the Netherlands and France went through from Group D. A brace from Portugal's Nuno Gomes sank Turkey in the first quarter-final, while Italy beat Romania by the same score-line in the second. The Netherlands then thrashed Yugoslavia 6-1 (including a Patrick Kluivert hat-trick and a Marc Overmars double), while the ever-improving French saw Spain off 2-1 (Raul missed a late penalty to save the game for the Spanish). Despite Gomes scoring again in the first semi-final, Portugal were eventually beaten by a controversial extra-time penalty from France's Zinedine Zidane at the newly renamed King Baudouin Stadium in Brussels. In the second semi, ten-man Italy eliminated the Netherlands on penalties, with reserve goalkeeper Francesco Toldo making two magnificent saves (he'd also saved a penalty in normal time that might have given the Dutch victory).

The meeting between France and Italy in the final of Euro 2000 at the Feyenoord stadium in Rotterdam in front of fifty thousand fans was clearly a match between the best teams in the tournament. With four minutes of injury time on the clock and the final whistle imminent, Marco Delvecchio must have thought his fifty-fifth minute goal was going to give Italy victory. But then France's Sylvain Wiltord blasted home from close range to take the match into extra time. Michel Platini had been the catalyst for France's victory in 1984 but this time it was Zinedine Zidane who provided the inspiration. He set up David Trezeguet to apply the finishing touch in the 103rd minute to give France a 2-1 Golden-Goal victory.

France and Italy line up before the final of Euro 2000

Fifty teams were divided into ten qualifying groups for Euro 2004 in Portugal. Teams that finished top of their group qualified automatically, while another five were selected after the runners-up played each other on a home and away basis. They then joined the hosts in a sixteen-team tournament. Although hosts Portugal lost their opening match to rank outsiders Greece, they won their next two matches and topped Group A. Greece and Spain finished with the same number of points and identical goal difference, but Greece had scored more so the Spanish failed to make it through to the knockout stages. France and England qualified comfortably from Group B at the expense of Switzerland and Croatia. England would have topped the group but for two injury-time strikes by Zidane. Although Bulgaria were thumped in Group C, Sweden, Denmark and Italy all finished with identical records. It was the Italians who dropped out however, as their goal difference was inferior. The Germans were the surprise casualties in Group D, with the Czech Republic and the Netherlands topping the table.

The hosts played England in the first quarter-final. Michael Owen opened the scoring early on but Sven-Göran Eriksson's side then made the familiar error of not pushing for a second and Postiga equalised with seven minutes left. In a repeat of what happened at the 1998 World Cup against Argentina, Sol Campbell thought he'd won the match with a header in the dying seconds, only for the referee to rule it out for a push on the goalkeeper. Both sides traded goals in extra time but Portugal won the penalty shoot-out 6-5, goalkeeper Ricardo saving Darius Vassell's spot-kick before scoring himself. Greece, meanwhile, were quietly progressing through the tournament. They defeated France 1-0 in their quarter-final, becoming the first team to beat hosts and holders in the event's history. Sweden and the Netherlands played out an entertaining 0-0 draw but it was the Dutch who progressed after a 5-4 victory on penalties. The Czech Republic then thrashed Denmark 3-0 to reach the semi-final. The hosts beat the Netherlands 2-1, a spectacular Maniche effort seeing them through to a final on home soil. The Czechs started their semi-final against Greece as overwhelming favourites and they hit the bar early on but, in the last moments of the first half of extra time, Traianos Dellas popped up to head home the Silver Goal winner (whereas a Golden Goal immediately ended the match, a Silver Goal, of which this is the only one ever to decide a major competitive match, meant that the team leading after the first half of extra time would be declared the winner). So the un-fancied Greeks took on the hosts in the final in Lisbon in front of sixty-three thousand, with Portugal hoping to avenge their opening-day defeat. The result proved that the so-called lesser teams were closing the gap on the super-powers of the world game. Despite being put under enormous pressure, the hard-working Greeks defended well and scored via an Angelos Charisteas header after an hour to seal a memorable 1-0 victory.

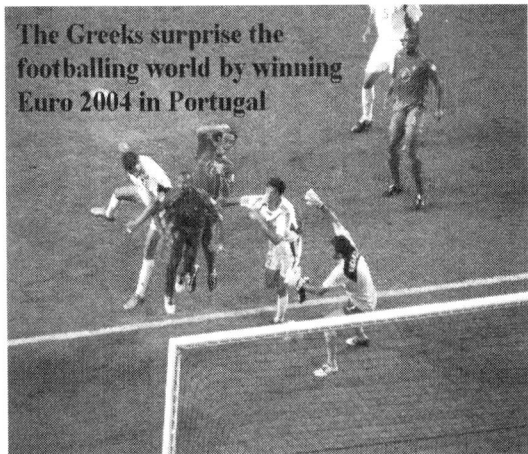

The Greeks surprise the footballing world by winning Euro 2004 in Portugal

Austria and Switzerland co-hosted the 2008 tournament, which featured a new trophy. The qualifying format was also changed, with the sixteen teams making it to the final competition comprising the winners and runners up from seven groups (fifty teams) along with the two host nations. Portugal and Turkey survived a tough Group A, from which the Czech Republic and co-hosts Switzerland were eliminated. Croatia and Germany then edged out Austria and Poland in Group B, while the Netherlands and Italy topped Group C. A strong Spanish side took Russia through with them from Group D, leaving defending champions Greece without a win and bottom of the table. England failed to qualify for the finals. The first quarter-final pitted Germany against Portugal. An exciting game was eventually won 3-2 by the Germans. Turkey played Croatia in the second match, with the Turks salvaging a draw deep into injury time at the end of extra time. The Croats then missed three penalties and Turkey went through to the semi-final. Russia took the lead against the Netherlands in the third quarter-final but Ruud van Nistelrooy equalized with five minutes to go. The Russians added two goals in extra time to advance to the semi-final. Spain and Italy played out one hundred and twenty goal-less minutes, but it was the Spanish who held their nerve in the shoot-out.

Turkey's luck finally ran out in front of forty thousand fans against the Germans in Basel in the first semi-final. The score was 1-1 at halftime, but they fell behind to a Miroslav Klose goal with ten minutes left. Although Semih Şentürk equalized in the eighty-sixth minute, Philipp Lahm fired the winner in injury time to give the Germans a 3-2 victory. In the second semi, Spain comprehensively dismantled Russia 3-0, with goals from Xavi, Daniel Güiza and David Silva. Spain, in their first final since they met France in Euro '84, took the lead against Germany at the Ernst Happel stadium in

Vienna through Fernando Torres.

The Germans dominated possession but couldn't break through solid Spanish defence and the Torres goal proved decisive. One hundred and eighty-four million euros was then paid out in prize money. Spain would later lift the 2010 World Cup in South Africa.

1

The venues for 2012

Eight cities with new or renovated stadiums across Poland and the Ukraine were used during the 2012 European Championships:

Poland

Warsaw

Spanning the Vistula River a hundred and sixty miles south of the Baltic Sea, the capital of Poland, known as the Phoenix city after its rise from the rubble of World War Two, has a population of just under two million. Legend has it that the city got its name from a fisherman, Wars, who fell in love with a mermaid, Sawa, in the Middle Ages, although its name actually means 'belonging to the Warsz people'.

Early settlements on the site were raided in the thirteenth century so a new community was founded around a fishing village called Warszowa. By the fourteenth century, Prince Boleslaw had established it as the seat of the Duke of Masovia and, a hundred years later, it was declared the capital of the region. It thrived on an economy based on trading the works and crafts of local people.

By 1530, the city had become the seat of the General Sejm (the lower house of the Polish Parliament) and by 1570 it had given its name to the Warsaw Confederation, which established religious freedom between Poland and Lithuania. King Sigismund Vasa III moved his court, and thus the Polish Crown, to Warsaw from Kraków in 1596 and the town quickly expanded to encompass many local districts.

The city was about to enter its first period of upheaval however. Between 1655 and 1658 it was besieged three times by Swedish and Transylvanian forces, and three times it capitulated and was ransacked. In 1700 it became embroiled in the Great North War, during which it was brought to its knees and ordered to pay compensation to the besieging forces. A hundred years of relative calm followed. Stanislav Poniatowski used this period to remodel the Royal Castle and declare the city a centre for European culture and the arts, and Warsaw soon became known as the 'Paris of the East'.

A second tumultuous era followed in the nineteenth century when it was annexed by the Kingdom of Prussia and demoted from its capital status to become the first city in southern Prussia. Napoleon promptly liberated the city in 1806 and, after the Congress of Vienna a decade later, Warsaw became a constitutional monarchy under a personal union with Imperial Russia. Although there were several uprisings in the mid-nineteenth century, the city flourished under Mayor Sokrates Starynkiewicz. He introduced a sewage system, street lights and gas works, and modernised the tramlines.

In 1918, immediately after declaring its independence, Warsaw was made the capital of Poland. The Russians saw this as an affront to their revolutionary ideals and invaded, but the city defended itself in the eastern suburbs and repelled the Red Army. It could not, however, fight back against the Nazi occupation in the Second World War, although the Warsaw Ghetto Uprising in 1943 held out for almost a month. When the city finally succumbed, two hundred thousand people, around a third of the population, were slaughtered

Eighty percent of Warsaw's buildings were destroyed in the Second World War.

as part of Hitler's Final Solution.

A second uprising in August 1944 was intended to oust the Germans before the Soviets arrived. After sixty-three days of heavy fighting, the native army and thousands of civilians once again capitulated. The Germans promptly destroyed around eighty-five percent of Warsaw and massacred two hundred thousand civilians. The Red Army finally came to the rescue in January 1945 but by then the city was in ruins.

The Soviets immediately set about rebuilding the city, erecting thousands of prefabricated buildings for the homeless. Although some gothic, renaissance, neoclassical and baroque architecture survived the war, many of Warsaw's streets and historic buildings were restored, and several new palaces were built. In the following years a growing anti-communist movement was led by Pope John Paul II, and a period of democratic change was ushered in throughout the 1980s. The biggest economic boom in its history saw the country accepted into the European Union in 2004.

The first match of the 2012 European Championships were held

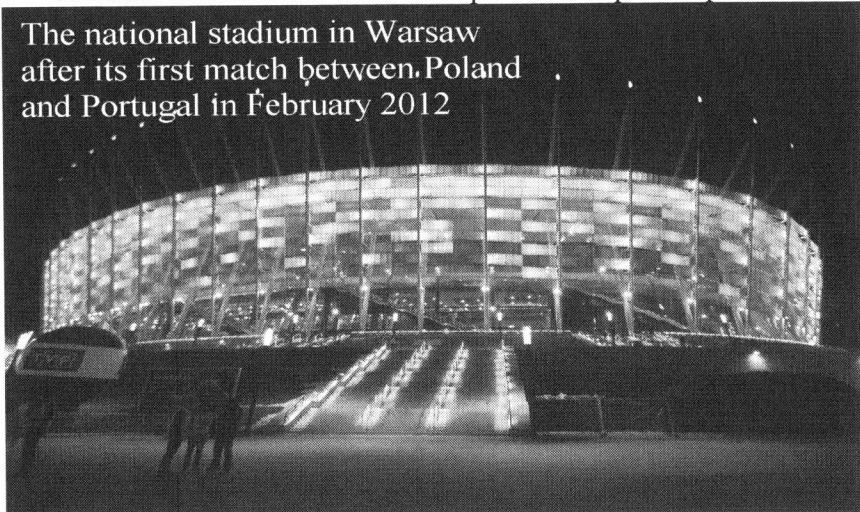

The national stadium in Warsaw after its first match between Poland and Portugal in February 2012

at the National Stadium in Warsaw. Completed in November 2011 at a cost of five hundred million euros, the state-of-the-art fifty-eight-thousand-capacity venue is part of an impressive sports complex that includes an enormous indoor arena, Olympic swimming pool, an aquatic park, hotel with conference centre, and dedicated railway and metro stations. Although it will be used primarily as a national football stadium, the two largest club sides in the city, Legia and Polonia, will use it for important Champions League or Europa League matches. It hosted two further group matches, one quarter-final and one semi-final during the tournament.

Gdańsk

Formerly known as Kdanzk, Danczk and Danzig, this city on the shores of the Baltic, with a population of around half a million, is the largest city in the Pomeranian district and the fifth largest in Poland. It is also the country's major seaport, which has made it a militarily strategic city throughout its long and turbulent history.

The original Pomeranian settlement was established in the seventh century but it was weak and wasn't fortified until Mieszko I linked this corner of the Polish state with the Baltic trade routes in 980. The town itself was founded in 997 (and celebrated its millennial anniversary in 1997) when Saint Adalbert of Prague baptized the population. The old Piast stronghold was eventually expanded to include German merchant settlements and the housing and workshops of craftsmen in the Long Market.

The town hall spire in the centre of Gdansk

Over the next three hundred years a monastery was added, it became the centre of a splinter duchy, was granted city status under Lübeck law in 1235, and grew to house a population of several thousand. In 1308, forces of the Holy Roman Empire under the moniker, the Margraviate of Brandenburg, laid siege to the city. King Wladyslaw I drafted in thousands of Teutonic knights to retake the city but they ended up slaughtering most of its inhabitants and displacing the native German and Kashubian settlers before colonising the area themselves. The knights built a fortress and established trade routes with Bruges, Novgorod and Seville.

The Polish-Teutonic Wars threatened to derail the city's expansion but the trade of wheat, timber and other goods along the River Vistula from central Poland and Prussia only increased its economic significance. A series of wars in the fifteenth century saw the city under Polish then Teutonic rule before the Prussian Confederation engaged in the war of independence and it became an autonomous city that was declared part of Poland. All trace of the knights was destroyed while new fortifications were built and new trading routes were established. The city's wealth and strategic position on the coast soon brought it to the attention of King Stephen Báthory and he surrounded it. The city's five thousand-strong army held out for six months but they were eventually defeated in December 1577. The city was forced to recognize Báthory as the ruler of Poland and had to pay an enormous 'apology' in gold.

There followed a period of relative calm before the Russians took control after another prolonged siege in 1734. Napoleon declared Danzig a free city in the early nineteenth century but, after his defeat in 1815, it became the capital of Western Prussia. It survived two revolutions in the middle of the century and then came under German rule in 1871. When Poland regained independence after the Great War, Danzig once again became a free city under the protection of the League of Nations, as long as it provided Poland with access to the Baltic. However, the majority of the population was German, and they campaigned vigorously to have the city reincorporated into the country. When Hitler came to power in 1933, he demanded the city be returned, but, when his demands were not met, he massed his forces and invaded anyway, dragging the entire continent into another war.

The turning point in the war came when Hitler split his forces in the hope of defeating east and west simultaneously. The Allies in the west counter-attacked on D-Day and the Russians pushed the Nazis back from the eastern front. By early 1945, the German army was in full retreat, with tens of thousands of refugees being forced towards Danzig in a repeat of the German advance on Dunkirk earlier in the war. Enormous numbers of troops and refugees were killed when Soviet submarines sunk German ships trying to escape and the Red Army finally captured the city in March.

The occupying Russians immediately set about rebuilding a city devastated by war, placing special emphasis on the strategic port. The communist regime was challenged during violent demonstrations in 1970, with the uprising slowly gathering pace so that by 1989 the Soviet influence was ousted by president-elect Lech Wałęsa's solidarity movement. In 2007, Gdańsk's Donald Tusk became prime minister of Poland. His native city is now a popular tourist destination and major shipping port. Its new football stadium, the PGE Arena, hosted several matches during the 2012 European Championships.

Completed in mid-2011, the forty-four-thousand-seat stadium was remodelled from its former self as the Baltic Arena. Costing around two hundred million euros, it is now a modern, amber-coloured dedicated football venue with forty-eight private boxes, one thousand five hundred VIP seats and fifty seats with better access to the stadium floor for disabled fans. The Polish Energy Group (PGE) bought the rights to the stadium's name for five years for around ten million euros. It hosted three group matches and one quarter-final.

The PGE Arena in Gdansk

Wroclaw

Lying on the River Oder, the city of Wroclaw, which has been part of Austria, Prussia and Germany, is now the largest conurbation in Poland's southwest, and it was the capital of the historic region of Silesia in the early twentieth century. A modest settlement of around a thousand people on the site of the current city (with over six hundred thousand inhabitants it is now the fourth largest in Poland) was recorded by Thietmar in 1000. By 1175 it had been known variously as Wrezlaw, Prezla and Breslaw, which morphed into the new German word Breslau in the fourteenth century. The traditional Polish name was thought to have originated from Vratislaus I of Bohemia however, who was also known as Wrocislaw.

In the tenth century the site was an important crossroads on the trading routes known as the Amber Road and the Via Regia or Royal Highway. The town initially came under the rule of Bohemia and the Kingdom of Poland, and, by the thirteenth century, it had become a political centre of a divided Poland. The Mongol invasion of Europe in 1241 left the city a burning wasteland but it was soon rebuilt by early German settlers and adopted the name Breslau. Timber houses sprang up in no time, the city adopted Magdeburg Rights, and it then joined the Hanseatic League under the Polish Piast Dynasty. It soon became part of Bohemia, which was itself a minion of the Roman Empire.

Two fires almost destroyed the city in the mid-fourteenth

century but it was immediately rebuilt. It took to Protestantism during the reformation in 1518 but Silesia was soon under the Catholic House of Habsburg. When the sides and their allies contested the Thirty Years' War, the city was occupied by opposing forces, of whom thousands were killed during an outbreak of Plague. After the counter-reformation, the city became a centre for German literature and poetry. Prussia then annexed most of Silesia and Habsburg Empress Maria Theresa renounced her claim to the territory in 1763.

The city was again occupied during the Napoleonic Wars and it soon became a haven for the German anti-Napoleonic movement. Prussian forces under Frederick William III gathered here before being mobilised against the French in the military campaign that ended with the Battle of Leipzig. This was the largest battle in Europe until the First World War and it effectively ended Napoleonic influence in Germany and Poland. Breslau prospered under German rule and the railways and new transport links ensured it became an important trading hub for cotton, precious metals and linen, and the new university meant it gained a reputation as a home of science and education. By the unification of Germany in 1871 it was the sixth largest city in the empire. After the Great War, it became the capital of Polish Silesia and expanded to house six hundred thousand inhabitants.

Most of the city's ten thousand Jews were sent to concentration camps in WWII, while the rest were rounded up and executed during the holocaust. The Red Army eventually liberated the war-torn city in May 1945 but by then half of it had been destroyed. Almost all the Germans were expelled by 1949 and the Polish government re-settled thousands of natives to rebuild the city.

The city's Municipal Stadium

In 1997 much of the city was flooded when the Oder burst its banks, but today Wroclaw is a vibrant and unique city with architecture reflecting its mixed-heritage past. The forty-three-thousand-seat Municipal Stadium in the city will host three group matches during Euro 2012. Built at a cost of one hundred and ninety million euros, the glass fibre and Teflon structure, which was completed in late 2011, also boasts a sports complex, VIP zone, outdoor promenade and train station.

Poznań

Spanning the Warta River in the central western region of Poland, the city, with a population of just over half a million, is the fifth largest in the country. As one of Poland's oldest cities, and an important centre for trade in its distant past, Poznań is said by its inhabitants to be the country's first capital. Its name probably derives from the old Polish verb poznać, which means 'to know'. Or it could be named after a person, Poznan, meaning one who is known or recognised.

Thietmar's chronicle lists a settlement on the site in the tenth century but it's likely there was a small town on the river dating back to the eighth century, and it crops up in various Latin documents over the next three hundred years. Mieszko I was apparently baptised in the fortified stronghold in 966 and it became the Polan tribe's most important cultural and political centre. Soon afterwards, construction began on the city's cathedral, and all of the Piast monarchs from Mieszko I to King Przemysl II were buried here.

After Mieszko II's death in the mid-eleventh century, the city was seen as weak and it was immediately invaded by Bretislaus I of Bohemia. Although he destroyed many of the buildings, Casimir the Restorer soon reunited Poland with Kraków as its capital. Over the next hundred years Poland was divided into duchies overseen by the king's sons, during which time the Royal Castle was built. Thomas of Guben was then instructed to bring in thousands of German labourers to expand the town around the castle but inside a defensive wall.

When Poland reunited in the Middle Ages, Poznań's importance grew steadily because it was on the east-west fur trading routes from Lithuania and Ruthenia to Germany and beyond. Despite being hit by regular fires (the castle was destroyed in 1536) and floods, the town continued to grow and it became an important seat of learning with the founding of a Jesuits' college in 1571. Because of its strategic position on the trade routes it became a target for rival forces (the Wars of Polish Succession and the Seven Years' War, to name but two) and looters in the eighteenth century. It was also decimated by Plague and more flooding, and the population declined from twenty thousand to just six thousand within a few decades.

During the second partition of the country in the latter years of the century, Poznań came under Prussian rule. The authorities encouraged migration and the city was soon expanding again, but, in the 1806 uprising, civilians and some of the military sided with Napoleon to drive the Prussians out. With Napoleon's defeat in 1815, however, the city was returned to Prussian rule and it became the capital of the Grand Duchy of Posen. The city's defences were strengthened once more and the railways arrived in 1848. The city was then incorporated into the German Empire after unification in 1871.

When the Treaty of Versailles divided Germany up after the First World War, Poznań became part of Poland and anyone not accepting citizenship was forced to leave. The interwar years brought relative calm to the region but the peace was short-lived and, under German occupation in WWII, Poznań was incorporated into the Third Reich. The city eventually fell to Soviet forces in February 1945 but the battle left much of it destroyed. With the city now almost exclusively inhabited by Poles, it became a voivodship capital, a status it had rescinded in 1975 during the country's reforms.

Poznań's Miejski Stadium under construction

Much of the city had to be rebuilt after the war and another wave of expansion began in the late 1980s. Following the failure of communism in 1990, the country held its first free and democratic elections. With the Euro 2012 football championships looming, Poznań extended its tram connections, built a motorway and completely renovated the City Stadium. The one hundred and sixty million-euro redevelopment project was completed in 2010 and increased the venue's capacity to forty-three thousand covered seats. The city hosted three group matches during the tournament.

Ukraine

Donetsk

With a population of nearly a million, and straddling the Kalmius River in the steppes to the east of the country, Donetsk is the fifth largest city in the Ukraine. Founded as recently as 1869 by Welsh steel and coal magnate, John Hughes, the city has been declared the unofficial capital of the Donets Basin.

Hughes founded a steel mill and several coal mines in the southern Russian Empire in the late nineteenth century and a town soon sprang up as workers were drafted in. Originally known as Hughesovka to westerners, the locals renamed the settlement Yuzovka (with Yuz being a Russian approximation of Hughes). In only forty years the population had swelled to fifty thousand. The city escaped the First World War unscathed but it soon fell under Soviet rule and was renamed Stalin, meaning steel, which was soon changed to Stalino.

With the construction of freshwater pipes and then a sewage system in the 1930s, the population exploded, and by the beginning of the Second World War it stood at over half a million. The Nazi invasion cut numbers by sixty percent and most of the city was completely destroyed during their two years of occupation. During their tenure, they introduced a system where for every German killed by civilians or the resistance, a hundred locals would be slaughtered. More than ninety-five thousand people were exterminated under this collective responsibility ruling.

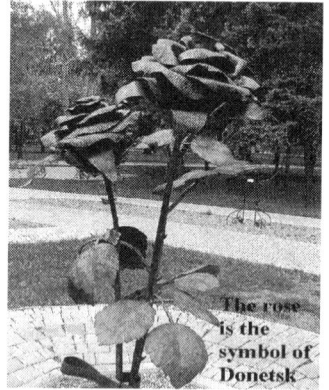

The rose is the symbol of Donetsk

At the end of the war, thousands of labourers were drafted in to rebuild the city and work its mines in an effort to raise currency, but conditions were terrible and hundreds died from malnutrition and disease. Stalin himself died in the early 1950s and the Soviet Union immediately fought to distance itself from his leadership. Nikita Krushchev immediately renamed the city Donetsh after a tributary of the local river.

A science academy was founded in 1965 and the city was awarded the Order of Lenin in 1979. Recent electoral problems have highlighted corruption at the highest level of government, but this appears to have been weeded out and the country is now enjoying a period of stability. Indeed the city has become a centre for culture and the arts, architecture and sport.

The city's ultra-modern fifty-one-thousand-capacity Donbass Arena was also used as part of the Euro 2012 football tournament. Built at a cost of three hundred million euros and opened with a Beyoncé concert in late 2009, the stadium (and the recreational park surrounding it), which is currently used by local side Shakhtar Donetsk, is in Lenin Comsomol Park in the city centre. It has a soaring roof designed to resemble a flying saucer and hosted group-stage games, as well as a quarter- and semi-final.

The magnificent Donbass Arena

Kharkiv

Founded in 1654 in the northeast of the country (at the confluence of three major rivers: Kharkiv, Lopan and Udy) as a centre for culture in the heart of the Russian Empire, it has since grown to become a vital administrative hub of the Kharkiv province. With a population approaching one and a half million, it is the second largest city in the Ukraine and is perhaps the most important seat of science, education, industry and transport in the region.

Recent archaeological discoveries tell us that the area had been home to tribal peoples since the Bronze Age nearly four thousand years ago. Later settlers from Scythia also populated the region and there's evidence supporting habitation by the Chernyakhov people between the second and sixth centuries AD.

It remained no more than a small settlement until the arrival of Kharko in the mid-seventeenth century, however. The fledgling city soon became the centre of the Sloboda Cossacks who built fortifications on the surface and escape passages deep underground. For its time, it was a modern, bustling city. The university was

29

founded in 1805 and, within a hundred years, it had running water, sewers, cobbled streets, electric lighting and railway connections. Its population during these years of rapid expansion grew by a factor of thirty.

The Bolsheviks established Kharkiv as the capital of the Ukrainian Socialist Soviet Republic but there was fierce opposition to this from Ukrainian nationals who wanted their capital in Kiev. The Russians exerted a little pressure (most dissenters simply disappeared) but the Stalinist purges continued when Ukrainian and Polish civilians protested against the iron rule of the union.

The Second World War brought more misery to the area and several key battles were fought around Kharkiv. The Germans advanced and took the city in late 1941, but the Red Army retaliated,

Kharkiv's Freedom Square

disastrously at first, and then successfully in early 1943. The Nazis recaptured the city a month later but it was finally liberated in August, although, as was the case with most contested cities during the conflict, most of it was destroyed and a good percentage of its people killed (thirty thousand Jews were murdered and dumped in a mass grave just outside the city).

After the war, Kharkiv was extensively remodelled. It is now known for its industry (the famous T-34 tank was designed and built

The Metalist Arena: Kharkiv

here), aerospace technology, nuclear turbines and rapid-transit metro system. It is also a major cultural centre boasting sixty scientific institutions, thirty colleges and universities, seven museums, eighty libraries and seven theatres. The city is football mad and hosts four teams. The revamped thirty-nine-thousand-seat Metalist Stadium (home to Metalist

30

Kharkiv) was chosen to stage several games at Euro 2012. The other teams are FC Kharkiv, FC Helios and FC Arsenal-Kharkiv.

Work on the original Metalist arena was begun in 1925 but it was a small municipal stadium that was enlarged to seat ten thousand in 1967. Since then it has undergone several more periods of renovation, most notably in 1974 when the new north and south stands raised capacity to thirty thousand, and again in the 1980s and 1990s when the east and south stands were rebuilt. The stadium underwent further construction work after being chosen to host the European Football Championships. The roof was replaced and several modernisation programs were ordered so it could re-open in 2009.

Lviv

A historically significant city on the River Poltva in the west of the Ukraine only seventy miles from Poland and a hundred miles from the Carpathian Mountains, Lviv is now an educational and cultural hotbed with its philharmonic orchestra, timeless buildings, machine industry and higher education establishments.

The area was home to early settlers by the fifth century, with the Lendian people claiming it as theirs by the turn of the millennium.

The historic old town of Lviv

They built a stronghold on the hill but it was captured by Vladimir I in 981. A town on the site was formerly established by King Daniel of Galicia (and named after his son Lev) in 1256 but it was invaded by the Tatars (ethnic Turks) at the behest of Mongol General Burundai only five years later. Much of the settlement was destroyed but Lev had rebuilt it by 1270 and it quickly expanded as Poles from Kraków were encouraged to migrate to the region. The territory was inherited by the Grand Duchy of Lithuania in 1340 and ruled by Dmitri Detko until the end of the decade.

King Casimir III then overran the city and built two new castles for protection. He also drafted in thousands of German workers and granted the city Magdeburg Rights. On Casimir's death, King Louis of Hungary inherited the kingdom and it was soon unified with the rest of Poland. It blossomed under the Roman Catholic Archdiocese from 1412 as it was granted exclusive trade rights, and it became a major trading centre on the routes between the Black Sea and Western Europe. Many merchants made the city their home so the population became increasingly ethnically diverse, incorporating Germans, Jews, Poles, Armenians and Ruthenians but, over time, they all united under the dominant Polish culture.

The seventeenth century was by no means as peaceful. Armies from Sweden, Hungary and the Russian Cossacks invaded but the city refused to fall. Indeed, it wasn't taken by hostile forces until well after the Ottoman siege of 1672, when Swedish troops under King Charles XII finally broke its resistance in 1704. Following the first partition of Poland at the end of the eighteenth century, the entire region was annexed by Austria and the city prospered, its population multiplying seven-fold over the next hundred years. To cater for the influx, the Austrians built a university, launched the city's first newspaper and pioneered the use of street lighting.

After the merger between the Austrian and Hungarian empires in 1867, the slide towards German culture and language was slowed and Polish, Ukrainian and Ruthenian became the major languages. The city was now home to the national library, the Polish Academy of Arts, the theatre and the archdiocese, and the Polish Historical Society, but it was equally dedicated to promoting and exporting Ukrainian ideals, language and culture.

Lviv was captured by the Russians at the beginning of the First World War but it was retaken by Austro-Hungary a year later. At the end of the war, the native Poles and Ukrainians took up arms against one another in a bid to claim the city as their own, with the Ukrainians declaring it their capital. Polish forces forced them out of the city but the Ukrainians promptly laid siege to Lviv. The Poles eventually won and pushed the Ukrainian army east to the River Zbruch. The Russians saw an opportunity to attack a city weakened by war but the Poles held out and their sovereignty over the area was accepted in 1923. To send a message to dissident Ukrainians, they closed down their schools and outlawed their language and culture.

At the beginning of WWII, German forces surrounded the city but the Red Army counterattacked and took it in the first month of the conflict. They re-opened Ukrainian schools and the language made a comeback, but it was short-lived. The Nazis invaded Russia in mid-1941 and the town fell again. They slaughtered the Poles and two hundred thousand Jews but viewed the Ukrainians as partly Aryan because of their subservience to the Austro-Hungarian Empire and they were treated leniently.

The Soviets liberated the city in 1944 and immediately incorporated it into the union, ousting the Polish population and pushing them west. A border agreement was then signed and Lviv formerly became part of Russia in February 1946. It grew rapidly in the following decades as it became an industrial hub. By the 1980s, the iron rule of its Soviet masters was a thing of the past and a movement for independence gathered pace. It was finally realised in August 1991. Today, Lviv and its eight hundred thousand inhabitants count themselves as a centre for culture and commerce in a modern and vibrant city.

Built at a cost of eighty-five million euros in the south of the city, the thirty-five-thousand-capacity New Stadium hosted three group games during Euro 2012. Construction began in 2007/8 and the arena and surrounding complex, with its transparent roof, VIP boxes, subterranean parking, media centre, restaurants, concert hall and training centre, was opened in 2011. The city's infrastructure, including its train and tram network, was extensively remodelled in time for the tournament.

Lviv's New Stadium

Kiev

Lying on the River Dnieper in the north of the country, Kiev, with its population of nearly three million, is the largest city in the Ukraine. Reportedly named after Kyi, a Slavic leader in the fifth century, the city is now a vibrant metropolis and the capital of the independent Ukraine.

There were numerous Slavic settlements in the region throughout the sixth and seventh centuries, and a small fortified stronghold was founded on the banks of the river in the late eighth century as an outpost for the Khazar Empire. During the next hundred years it was ruled by the Varangians, the Magyars and then by Oleg after his invasion in 882. Several hundred years of peace followed but the city was razed to the ground by Prince Rostislavic of the Kipchaks in 1203. Despite being partially rebuilt, and claiming to be the largest city in the world with a population exceeding one hundred thousand, it was completely eradicated by Batu Khan when his Mongol army invaded in 1240.

For the next two hundred years the city was fought over by the Lithuanians, the Tatars and the Poles, but it was eventually ceded to the Grand Duchy of Lithuania and the Polish-Lithuanian Commonwealth until the mid-seventeenth century. It then became an autonomous city under vague Russian rule. During this time the city developed into a cradle for pilgrims, religious leaders and businessmen looking to exploit the area's natural resources.

Russian migration throughout the eighteenth and nineteenth centuries all but eradicated the Ukrainian and Slavic influence, with the former being marginalised in the city's outskirts. The industrial revolution saw their presence in the city increase as they used the river to transport sugar and grain to the major trade routes. Factories sprang up and the population boomed until there were more than a quarter of a million people living in Kiev by 1900.

After the First World War, the city became the capital of a number of fledgling states but it was keenly contested during the Polish-Soviet War and the latter's civil war, and it changed hands repeatedly. In that time, the Ukrainian people and language became the dominant influence on society and culture and, in 1934, Kiev was named as the capital of the Soviet Ukraine. It grew as an industrial town and as a centre for science and technology, but the two years of German occupation during the Second World War all but destroyed it. The Ukrainian underground firebombed German military headquarters so they retaliated by rounding up the entire Jewish population and massacring them at Babi Yar.

The city was eventually liberated by the Red Army and it recovered quickly after the end of hostilities. By the 1970s it was the third largest conurbation in the Soviet Empire. Tragedy struck in 1986 when the Chernobyl nuclear power station was destroyed in an explosion but, thankfully, prevailing winds took the radioactive fallout away from the city. Having declared independence from the Soviet Union in 1991, Ukraine named Kiev as its capital.

The Olympic Stadium in the heart of the city was originally built in the 1920s and known as the Red Stadium of Trotsky. It underwent several name changes and periods of renovation in the intervening years but now, with a capacity of around seventy thousand, it is known as the Olympic NSC (national sports complex). Local side Dynamo used to use the stadium but declining attendances, except during high-profile international games, forced them to move to the Lobanovski Stadium instead. The Olympic complex will host the final of the Euro 2012 tournament on July 1st.

Kiev's Olympic Stadium

2

The teams for 2012

Poland

The co-hosts of the 2012 European Football Championships will celebrate their international centenary in 2019. Although founded in Warsaw just after the end of the First World War, the Polish national team – known as the Red and Whites or the White Eagles – would have to wait two years for their first official match when they played Hungary in Budapest. They lost 1-0 and would have to wait another year to record their first victory after a close match against Sweden in Stockholm (2-1). The side failed to qualify for the 1930 World Cup in Uruguay or the next tournament in Italy, but they thrashed Yugoslavia to ensure qualification for the 1938 finals in France.

They were drawn against Brazil, a side that was not as feared as it is today but which was still one of the major forces in world football. The Poles took the South Americans to extra time, with four goals from Ernest Wilimowski, but they eventually lost a thrilling encounter 6-5. Despite crashing out of the tournament, they played a one-off match against the World Cup runners-up, Hungary, just before the outbreak of WWII. They announced themselves on the international scene by winning 4-2.

The post-war years were marked by glorious highs and humiliating lows. They beat the superb Czechs 3-1, then lost 8-0 to an ordinary Danish side. In the early 1960s they banished the memory with a 9-0 demolition of Norway. This remained their record victory until they thumped San Marino 10-0 in 2009. Polish football really came of age in the 1970s and early 1980s however, when Kazimierz Górski was elected as their coach. Only two years after taking charge he guided the side to the gold medal at the 1972 Olympics in Munich, and, in 1974, the team shocked the football world by making the semi-final of the World Cup in Germany. The other teams should have been prepared for their speed and ability, and need only have taken a look at their performances in qualifying when they knocked out a very strong England.

In their opening match of the World Cup proper, they dispatched

South American giants Argentina 3-2 before thrashing Haiti 7-0 in their next game. They then beat 1970 runners-up Italy 2-1 to cap an incredible first round. In the knockout stages they saw off Sweden (1-0) and Yugoslavia (2-1). In terrible conditions that nullified their speed and agility, they lost 1-0 to eventual champions Germany in the semi-final. Despite the disappointment, they lifted themselves to beat Brazil 1-0 in the third/fourth play-off. They then took the silver medal at the 1976 Montreal Olympics.

Although they progressed to the second round at the 1978 World Cup in Argentina, they lost to the hosts (and eventual winners) 2-0 before being soundly beaten by Brazil 3-1. They started the next World Cup in Spain slowly, with goal-less draws against eventual winners Italy and Cameroon, but they then thrashed Peru 5-1, the incomparable Grzegorz Lato netting yet again (he'd been their star man in 1974). The other first round results meant that they surprisingly topped their group and went on to face Belgium, where a Zibi hat-trick saw them home 3-0. They then drew against the Soviet Union before losing to Italy in the semi-final (2-0). Polish football's golden era finally came to an end with a 3-2 victory over France in the play-off. They reached the knockout stages of Mexico '86 but were humiliated 4-0 by Brazil (it was the last World Cup for which Poland qualified until 2002).

There was the odd high point in the intervening years, a silver medal at the 1992 Barcelona Olympics being one, but the core of the great side had all retired and this generation was not able to make an impact on the international stage. They qualified for the World Cup in the Far East in 2002 but were humbled by co-hosts South Korea 2-0 before being thumped 4-0 by Portugal. A 3-1 win against the

USA in their last group match couldn't save them from being dumped out of the tournament. The suffered a similar fate in Germany in 2006, losing their first two games and winning their last, but, again, it was not enough.

The side made its first appearance in the European Championships in Austria and Switzerland in 2008 but they had a disappointing tournament and were eliminated without a win. They couldn't raise themselves for the qualifying matches for South Africa 2010 and duly failed to make it to the finals. However, in 2007, Poland and the Ukraine were chosen to co-host Euro 2012. Both countries were forced to make huge changes to their infrastructure to cater for fans and the media, and they rebuilt or renovated four stadiums each to host the event.

Ukraine

Although the Ukrainian side only officially came into existence following the break-up of the Soviet Union in 1990, a representative Yellow-Blues side had been around since the 1920s, but it was not recognised internationally and was disbanded in 1935. Their last two matches were played against Prague and Moscow, with famous players like Privalov and the Fomin brothers then being forced to retire. Over the next sixty years, the best players from the Ukraine represented the Soviet Union. As soon as the union was dissolved, the Ukrainian Football Federation founded its own national team, although the side wasn't registered in time to enter the qualifying tournament for the 1994 World Cup in the USA.

Somewhat surprisingly, a few senior players (Andrei Kanchelskis, Oleg Salenko and Sergei Yuran) chose to play for the CIS Russian team rather than represent their new country. The national team played its first official game against Hungary in 1992 but it wasn't until 2006 that they qualified for a major tournament (Croatia beat them to a spot at France '98, Slovenia went through to Euro 2000 at their expense, Germany prevented them from making it to the 2002 World Cup, and qualifying for Euro 2004 went poorly).

Under new coach Oleg Blokhin, and with star players like Andriy Shevchenko, Sergei Rebrov and Anatoli Tymoshchuk, the side drew with Georgia in their final qualifying match and made it through to the 2006 World Cup in Germany. They were soundly thumped 4-0 by Spain in their opening match but they recovered to beat both Tunisia and Saudi Arabia to reach the knockout stages. After a 0-0 draw with Switzerland, the game went to the dreaded penalty shoot-out, but the Ukraine came through comfortably (3-0). They faced eventual champions Italy in the quarter-final and were beaten 3-0, but it had been a successful tournament for both the players and fans.

The high point of a World Cup quarter-final was followed by a crushing low when they only finished fourth in their qualification group for the 2008 European Championships. They finished second in their next World Cup group but then lost a play-off against Greece. As co-hosts for Euro 2012 with Poland, the trauma of qualifying has been avoided and the home side is expected to do well. A series of challenging friendly matches against top opposition – including Uruguay, the Czech Republic and Germany – was organised to prepare the team for the championships. Indeed, early 2011 saw the team put in a number of strong performances: the side won a Cyprus invitational tournament, beating Sweden, Romania and Chile in the process.

Coach Oleg Blokhin returned in 2011 for his second spell in

Andriy Shevchenko celebrates his goal against Sweden at Euro 2012

charge of the national team. Up front, former captain Andrei Shevchenko was recalled before the tournament. His forty-eight goals in one hundred and eleven caps remain Ukrainian records but he bowed out after the event.

Although their highest FIFA World Ranking was eleven in early 2007, the side has now slipped to thirty-first. They play most of their games at the National Sports Complex in Kiev. The team's biggest wins came against Azerbaijan in 2006 and Andorra in 2009 (6-0). They have twice been defeated 4-0, by Croatia in 1995 and Spain in 2006.

France

The national football team, which would soon operate under the

39

jurisdiction of the French Football Federation, played its first match in 1904, just before the founding of the international governing body, FIFA. In front of only five hundred spectators at the Parc des Princes stadium, France beat neighbouring Switzerland 1-0. The French sports union immediately claimed the team as their own and so began a long-running dispute with FIFA over the side's identity, the latter claiming it would be responsible for the team's entry at each Olympic Games.

The argument was resolved in the 1920s when the French sports union merged with the football federation, and the team travelled to Uruguay for the first World Cup with high hopes. Lucien Laurent scored the first goal in World Cup history as France demolished Mexico 4-1 in their first outing. They later lost to Argentina and Chile and were eliminated at the group stage, however. They fared no better at the second event in 1934 and were eliminated in the opening match by Austria.

They were chosen as hosts for the 1938 tournament and won their first match against Belgium, but they were then eliminated by Italy in the quarter-final. The continent was immediately dragged into war and most international sporting events were cancelled. By the 1950 World Cup in Brazil, the French national side was developing into a potent force.

Scotland and Turkey withdrew from the competition, the former because they hadn't won the home nations championship and the latter for financial reasons, so France and Portugal were invited instead, even though they hadn't qualified conventionally. France initially accepted but then withdrew because of the excessive travel times involved. Four years later in Switzerland they beat Mexico but lost to Yugoslavia and didn't make it past the group stage.

By the 1958 tournament in Sweden, France had come of age. In Just Fontaine and Raymond Kopa they had two of the stars of the event, the former scoring a hat-trick in a 7-3 demolition of Paraguay in their opening match. Although Fontaine scored two more, the French were uncharacteristically poor in their next match and they lost 3-2. They bounced back well, however, and both men were on the score-sheet again in a comfortable victory over Scotland which saw them top their group.

The incomparable Fontaine scored another brace in an easy win over Northern Ireland in the quarter-final but, despite another goal in the semi-final, France were not good enough to beat the Brazil of Pelé (who scored a hat-trick), Garrincha, Didi and Vavá. They ended the tournament on a high, however, as Fontaine scored another four in a 6-3 victory in the third/fourth playoff against West Germany. His tally of thirteen goals remains a record for a single tournament

The incomparable Just Fontaine scored 30 goals for France in just 21 appearances

and, with the tighter defences and superior goalkeeping of today's football, it is a record that is unlikely to be beaten (it took the majestic Brazilian Ronaldo three tournaments to match it).

The French then hosted the inaugural European Championships in 1960. In the opening round they'd dispatched Greece 8-2 on aggregate, and then a Fontaine hat-trick and another goal from Kopa saw them overcome Austria 9-4 in the two-legged quarter-final. Despite leading 3-1 and 4-2 against Yugoslavia in the semi-final in Paris, France conceded three goals in the last fifteen minutes and lost. They were then beaten by the Czechs in the playoff and eventually finished fourth.

France then entered a low period in their football history. The side failed to qualify for the 1962 World Cup or the next European Championships. They did reach the finals of the 1966 World Cup in England but they didn't win a game and finished bottom of a strong group that included the hosts and eventual champions. The 1970s would prove equally bleak, the national side failing to qualify for the World Cups in Mexico or Germany, or the European Championships in 1968, 1972, 1976 or 1980.

Although they did make it to Argentina for the 1978 World Cup, the side lost to Italy and the hosts – who would be the eventual champions – and only managed a consolation win over Hungary that couldn't prevent their elimination at the group stage.

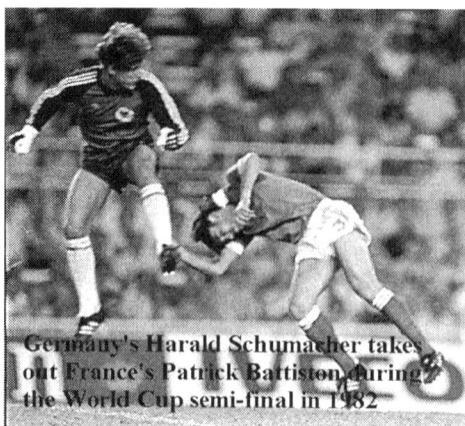

Germany's Harald Schumacher takes out France's Patrick Battiston during the World Cup semi-final in 1982

Hope was rekindled with the arrival of new coach Michel Hidalgo and a second golden generation of players like Michel Platini, Jean Tigana, Luis Fernández and Alain Giresse. They patrolled the pitch in what became known as the 'carré magique' or magic square which was an attacking variation of the Dutch total football system of the previous decade. This strong side was beaten by England in its first group match at the 1982 World Cup in Spain but good results against Czechoslovakia and Kuwait saw them qualify for the second phase. The latter match was dominated by a curious refereeing decision which ultimately cost Miroslav Stupar his job. France were leading 3-1 when Alain Giresse skipped past the last defender and scored what looked to be a perfectly good goal. But the Kuwaitis claimed they had head heard a whistle and had stopped playing. When Stupar signalled that the goal should stand, the president of the Kuwaiti football association, Sheikh Fahid Al-Ahmad Al-Sabah, raced down from the stand and confronted him on the pitch. To the disbelief of the French team, Stupar then reversed his initial decision and disallowed the goal. Sheikh Al-Sabah was fined ten thousand dollars for coming onto the pitch and Stupar had his referee's licence revoked. France eventually won the match 4-1.

France then beat Austria (1-0) and Northern Ireland (4-1) to reach their first semi-final since 1958. The match against West Germany was memorable for more than the football. Pierre Littbarski put the Germans ahead but Michel Platini equalised from the spot a few minutes later. Then came the game's most controversial moment: French defender Patrick Battiston raced clear of the German defence and poked the ball past the approaching German goalkeeper, Harald Schumacher. With the goal at his mercy it appeared that all Battiston had to do was sidestep the goalkeeper and roll the ball into the empty net but Schumacher had other ideas. He jumped at the defender to block him, the impact so serious that Battiston lost two teeth, suffered a broken jaw, broke two vertebrae and was knocked unconscious. The referee then inexplicably awarded a goal kick instead of sending Schumacher off for what was probably the worst foul in the history of the game. Manuel Amoros could have won the match for the French late on but his shot rebounded off the bar and it went to extra time.

Immediately after the break Marius Trésor beat Schumacher from close range, and Giresse made it 3-1 a few minutes later. Karl-Heinz Rummenigge pulled one back just before halftime and Klaus Fischer volleyed in the equaliser ten minutes from the end. It finished 3-3 and thus became the first match at the World Cup to be decided by penalties. Schumacher then stepped up to save Maxine Bossis's strike, which, when Horst Hrubesch scored, sent France crashing out of the tournament. Although Poland then beat them in the third/fourth playoff, the French were showing signs of once again becoming a dominant force in European football.

The country was chosen to host a Euro '84 tournament that saw several changes to the format to bring the championships into the modern era. Group winners and runners-up met in a pair of semi-finals and the playoff match was dropped because it was seen as a non-event. Michel Platini was the star of the tournament. He scored two hat-tricks and goals in every other game as France beat Denmark (1-0), thrashed Belgium (5-0) and then saw off Yugoslavia (3-2).

The semi-final against Portugal has been listed as one of the greatest international matches ever played. France took an early lead but Portugal equalised late on and sent the game into extra time. Rui Jordão then scored his second to give Portugal a surprise lead but Jean-François Domergue then got his second. The match looked to be heading for penalties when Platini fired a last-minute winner to see them through to a final against neighbours Spain. The final will be remembered for a horrible moment for Spanish goalkeeper Luis Arconada. He let a Platini free-kick squirm under his body which gave the French the lead. Despite counterattacking against the ten-man French, the Spanish could not find the net and Bruno Bellone scored in the last minute to give the hosts a 2-0 victory. The same side then won the Olympic gold in Los Angeles before completing a remarkable year by winning the Artemio Franchi trophy, which was the forerunner of the Confederations Cup.

France were still a force to be reckoned with two years later at the World Cup in Mexico. A Jean-Pierre Papin goal saw them beat Canada before they drew with eventual group winners, the Soviet

Union. They then demolished Hungary in their last group game so set up a meeting with reigning world champions Italy in the first round of the knockout stages. Goals from Michel Platini and Yannick Stopyra saw off the Italians at the Olympic Stadium in Mexico City and France were through to a quarter-final against Brazil.

Careca gave the South Americans the lead but Platini equalised from a cross just before halftime. French goalkeeper Joël Bats made up for an error late in the second half when he saved the resulting penalty from Zico and the match went to extra time. France were now the better side but they couldn't turn pressure into goals and the match went to the dreaded penalty shootout. Socrates and the usually solid Platini missed theirs before Julio Cesar struck the post. Luis Fernández then stepped up and put France in the semi-final. Andreas Brehme put the West Germans 1-0 up and Rudi Völler sealed the game with their second in the dying moments but the tournament had been a great success for France (they beat Belgium 4-2 in the playoff match to finish third) and they were tipped to do well at the 1988 European Championships in Germany.

Despite the opening of a national football institute and the appointment of Michel Platini as head coach, the side performed uncharacteristically poorly for the next two years and failed to qualify for the European Championships or the 1990 World Cup in Italy. Platini was given the benefit of the doubt, however, and the side went on a nineteen-match unbeaten run in the lead-up to Euro '92 in Sweden. Sadly they could not repeat this form at the finals themselves. They drew 1-1 with Sweden in their opening match, and they drew again with England in Malmö four days later. They were then beaten by the tournament's wildcards (and eventual winners), Denmark, in their last group game and they failed to reach the knockout stages.

Platini stepped aside in favour of Gérard Houllier for the qualifying tournament for USA '94. The side was in a strong position going into the last two matches against Israel and Bulgaria but they imploded in both matches, losing the former 3-2 and the latter 2-1. Houllier was immediately fired and several players were omitted from the squad by incoming coach Aimé Jacquet. He soon revived the national team and led them across the Channel for Euro '96 in confident mood.

France beat Romania in their opening match and they then drew with Spain at Elland Road, Leeds. They easily overcame Bulgaria (3-1) in their final match and topped their group. Their quarter-final against the Dutch at Anfield was a dull affair and they eventually progressed on penalties after Clarence Seedorf missed from the spot. The semi-final against the Czech Republic at Old Trafford was another drab game with no goals in the first two hours. This time it was the French who were unlucky, Reynald Pedros's spot kick being easily saved by Petr Kouba. Despite the negative tactics employed by some teams, the likes of Zidane and Dugarry showed that this new France would be around for some time and would certainly be a threat on home soil at the 1998 World Cup.

Lilian Thuram is France's most-capped player with 142 international appearances

France dominated their group, beating South Africa 3-0 in Marseille, Saudi Arabia 4-0 in Paris (despite a red card for Zidane for stamping on an opponent) and Denmark 2-1 in Lyon. The hosts almost came unstuck against Paraguay in the first knockout match in Lens but a Golden Goal from Laurent Blanc six minutes before the end of extra time broke South American hearts. They then squeezed past Italy after a penalty shootout in the quarter-final before Lilian Thuram stepped up to score two vitals goals (the only times he found the net for the national team in his hundred and forty-two caps) against Croatia in the semi-final. The Brazilian team were clearly concerned for team-mate Ronaldo after he'd suffered a seizure in the build-up to the final and France ran out comfortable (3-0) winners at the Stade de France in Paris.

The core of the side that won the World Cup was still available for selection for the qualifying tournament for Euro 2000 and France easily made it to the finals in Belgium and the Netherlands by topping their group. They promptly thrashed Denmark in their opening game before seeing off a strong Czech side 2-1. They lost their final group match against the Dutch but qualified for the knockout stages by finishing second in the table with six points. Zinedine Zidane gave the French the lead against Spain in the quarter-final but Gaizka Mendieta equalised from the spot a few minutes later. Youri Djorkaeff then scored the winner just before halftime so set up a semi-final against the tournament's surprise package, Portugal.

Portugal took the lead but Thierry Henry equalised just after halftime. The game went to extra time and Zidane won it with a Golden Goal penalty two minutes from the end. The French were staring defeat in the face in the final when Sylvain Wiltord scored in the fourth minute of injury time to equalise Marco Delvecchio's earlier strike. And they needed another Golden Goal, this time from David Trezeguet, to snatch the trophy in the first period of extra time. In so doing, they became the first side to hold both the World Cup and European Championship trophies.

With much of the same side still available after their 2001 Confederations Cup triumph, France were expected to put all-comers to the sword at the 2002 World Cup in Japan and Korea. They qualified automatically as champions and were drawn in a group alongside Senegal, Uruguay and Denmark. The French then inexplicably imploded. They failed to score a single goal and only managed a point from their match with Uruguay. It was the worst performance by the defending champions in the history of the event as they lost to Senegal and Denmark and were eliminated.

Under new coach Jacques Santini they won all eight of their qualifying games for Euro 2004 – scoring twenty-nine goals and conceding just two – and they entered the tournament as one of the favourites. They qualified from a strong group with a last-gasp victory over the English, a 2-2 draw against Croatia and a comfortable win over neighbours Switzerland. They then met the un-fancied Greeks in the quarter-final and were eliminated by an Angelos Charisteas goal midway through the second half. It was a bitter blow for a side expected to win the tournament, although the Greeks carried on surprising themselves and others and went on to win the trophy.

The side was struggling to qualify for the 2006 World Cup in Germany so new coach Raymond Domenech convinced some of the recent retirees to postpone their decision and rejoin the international squad. With qualification secured in their last match, they then made hard work of progressing from what should have been a relatively

46

easy group at the finals themselves. They drew with Switzerland and South Korea before beating Togo to make it to the knockout stages. They went 1-0 down to Spain but rallied with goals from Franck Ribéry, Patrick Vieira and Zinedine Zidane to set up a quarter-final against holders Brazil.

Zidane was inspirational and it was he who provided the cross for Thierry Henry to win the match and book a semi-final berth against Portugal. This time Zidane scored and France were through to another World Cup final. He opened the scoring against Italy from the penalty spot but Marco Materazzi equalised shortly afterwards. Both teams pushed hard for a winner but the game went to extra time. Zidane was then sent off for head-butting Materazzi and France lost the shootout that followed.

The qualifying campaign for Euro 2008 in Switzerland went well, despite two 1-0 losses to Scotland, and they finished second in their group behind Italy. The tournament was a different matter however. They were drawn in a 'group of death' along with Italy (ranked number one in Europe), the Netherlands (ranked fourth) and Romania (ranked twelfth). The French began their tournament with a dull 0-0 draw with Romania, and they were then thrashed 4-1 by eventual group winners, the Netherlands. This left France having to beat Italy to qualify for the knockout stages. Éric Abidal was sent off in the first half and Andrea Pirlo scored the penalty; then Daniele de Rossi added a second with half an hour to go and France were eliminated.

The qualifying campaign for the 2010 World Cup in South Africa stuttered but eventually yielded second place behind Serbia with twenty-one points from their ten games. This put the French into a playoff with the Republic of Ireland. The French won the first leg at Croke Park but the Irish fought back well at the Stade de France and took the lead through Robbie Keane. With the aggregate score tied at 1-1, the game went to extra time. In the last minute of the first half, Thierry Henry twice controlled the ball with his hand to stop it going out of play before crossing for William Gallas to head home the winner from close range. The Irish protested vehemently but the goal was allowed to stand.

Henry immediately said that the ball had hit his hand but he played on because the referee had not seen the infringement and called a halt to play. Some time after the match, he issued a statement saying he was embarrassed at how the game had ended

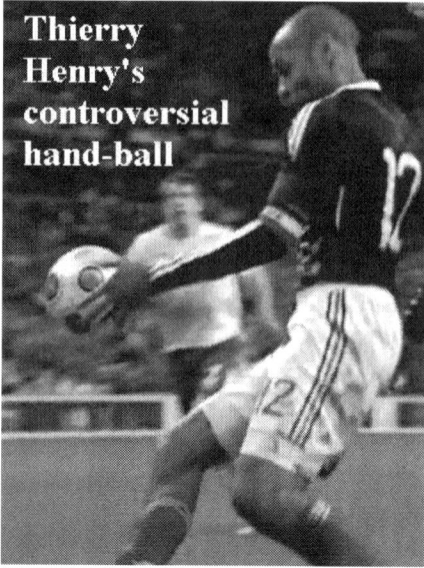

Thierry Henry's controversial hand-ball

and the fairest thing to do would be to replay the match. This was seen by some as an attempt to save face: when the ball went in, he'd celebrated wildly. In a phone call to Sepp Blatter over the incident, Henry said his family had been threatened by disgruntled fans.

Referee Martin Hansson came in for an enormous amount of stick and considered retiring, even though replays showed that it was impossible for him to have seen the handball. He later admitted to watching the incident on television and crying at the magnitude of the error he and his officials had made. His decision probably cost Ireland a place at the World Cup and the match was not replayed as FIFA repeatedly stated the referee's decisions in the game are final, no matter if they are right or wrong.

The tournament itself seemed to give credence to the view that France were either brilliant or awful: World Cup finalists in 1998 and 2006 and World Cup failures in 2002 and 2010. They could only draw with Uruguay before losing 2-0 to Mexico. In their last match they had to beat hosts South Africa to have any chance of making the knockout stages but they were beaten 2-1, goals from Khumalo and Mphela sending the French crashing out with no wins and only a single goal scored. That there had been disharmony in the camp throughout was highlighted when Nicolas Anelka was sent home by coach Raymond Domenech after a much-publicised bust up. The remaining players came out in support of Anelka and boycotted their next training session in what had become a shambolic camp.

The French needed to bounce back with a solid qualifying campaign for Euro 2012 in Poland and the Ukraine. They were drawn in a group that appeared relatively easy on paper but they promptly lost their first match to Belarus in the Stade de France. The side recovered from this early setback with 2-0 wins over Bosnia & Herzegovina, Romania and Luxemburg (home and away). They drew with Belarus second time out, then beat Albania, drew with

Romania and thrashed Albania 3-0 in Paris. They needed a draw with Bosnia & Herzegovina in their last match to finish top of their group and duly delivered at the Stade de France.

Just when it seemed the French team was stabilising, investigative website Mediapart issued a claim that the French Football Federation had tried to implement a race-quota system to limit the number of dual-citizenship players attending its academies. The website went on to suggest that this limit had been set at thirty percent and that, if it was met, no more non-white players would be allowed in the twelve to thirteen age bracket. The FFF denied the report but did suspend technical director François Blaquart while it carried out its own investigation.

In April 2011, team manager Laurent Blanc denied all knowledge of such practices at a press conference, but Mediapart immediately announced it had a recording of the meeting at which the race-quota subject had been raised. Blanc was forced to admit that he had made remarks that could have offended but denied he was racist and strongly defended the team's anti-discrimination policy. Lilian Thuram and Patrick Vieira were appalled when they heard the evidence and the French government was forced to step in to calm the camp down. With the backing of former team-mates Zidane, Deschamps, Dugarry and Petit, amongst others, Blanc was eventually exonerated and continued in his role as head coach of the national team.

France played two friendly matches against the United States and Belgium in November 2011 by way of warm-up games before Euro 2012. They beat the United Sates but could only manage a goal-less draw against the neighbouring Belgians.

The Republic of Ireland

For its first forty years, Ireland was represented by one team, which came under the jurisdiction of the Irish Football Association based in Belfast. In 1920 the country was divided into Northern Ireland and what became known as the Irish Free State, which then became Éire or, simply, Ireland under a new constitution in 1937. The Irish Free State side made its international debut at the Paris Olympics in 1924. They first defeated Bulgaria and made it to the quarter-final.

They then beat the United States but lost to Italy in their next match, and then only played sporadically before entering the qualifying tournament for the 1934 World Cup. At Dalymount Park they drew 4-4 with Belgium, the game all the more notable because Paddy Moore scored all four, thus becoming the first man to do so in a World Cup game.

In the 1930s the Irish Free State name began to fall out of use and the team simply became Ireland, but the two national football associations then became embroiled in a squabble because they both wanted to pick players from the whole island. The situation became so complicated that when the two teams qualified for the 1950 World Cup, some players had represented both nations. FIFA intervened and divided player eligibility by the political border and insisted that neither team be known as Ireland during tournaments. The south was therefore known as The Republic of Ireland, and the north, Northern Ireland.

In the build-up to the World Cup itself, they beat England but could not progress. They then drew with them in the qualifying tournament for the 1958 World Cup, two highlights of rather a drab decade for the side. They didn't qualify for the 1960 European Championships (this was the era when only four teams made it through the qualifying tournament to the finals proper) but they did reach the quarter-final stage of the following event. Despite having failed to qualify for a single World Cup, the side was given a chance to make the 1966 tournament in England when Syria withdrew from their pool. They beat Spain at home but lost away so were forced into a playoff against the same side. The match was held in Paris but the Spanish won 1-0.

The side struggled to find consistent form in the late 1960s and early '70s but they improved considerably with the arrival of star playmaker Liam Brady and player/coach Johnny Giles. With Brady the focal point for an improving squad, they narrowly missed out on qualifying for Argentina '78 even though they beat the mighty French. They beat them again in the next qualifying tournament but lost out on goal difference. New manager Eoin Hand was replaced after a poor run during the 1980s when they failed to make it to the 1984 European Championships or the 1986 World Cup in Mexico.

The arrival of Englishman Jack Charlton at the helm in 1986 saw a remarkable about-turn in their fortunes. The side qualified for Euro '88 by topping their group and then a Ray Houghton header saw off England 1-0 in the tournament proper. They then drew with the Soviet Union and looked to be on course for a semi-final spot before a late goal from the Dutch saw the Netherlands scrape through instead. Their good form continued into the qualification tournament for Italia '90 and they made the finals having beaten Spain, Northern Ireland, Hungary and Malta. They could only draw their three pool matches in Italy but that saw them through to a knockout match against Romania. Packie Bonner made a vital penalty save and, with David O'Leary converting his spot-kick, the Irish were through to a quarter-final against the hosts. It was no disgrace to lose 1-0 in Rome's Olympic Stadium.

Robbie Keane is the republic's captain and he holds the record for the most goals for his country with 54

The side remained unbeaten during qualifying for the 1992 European Championships but couldn't accumulate enough points to make the finals themselves, although their strong showing saw them through to the next World Cup in the USA. They avenged their defeat to Italy in their first match, a wonderful Ray Houghton strike sealing victory. They progressed to the knockout stages from a difficult group but eventually lost to the Netherlands. The most successful period in the side's history drew to a close with failure to qualify for Euro '96 in England.

Under new manager Mick McCarthy the side endured a few years in the sporting doldrums before qualifying strongly for the World Cup in the Far East in 2002. Despite losing their captain Roy Keane (a furious public argument with the manager saw Keane sent home in disgrace), the Republic made it to the knockout stages but were defeated by Spain on penalties. After McCarthy's departure

Brian Kerr and Steve Staunton couldn't take the side to the 2004 or 2008 European Championships or the 2006 World Cup.

The arrival of manager Giovanni Trapattoni saw another upsurge in their fortunes. They narrowly missed out on qualifying for the 2010 World Cup (Thierry Henry's handball providing the main talking point in the controversial playoff against France) but performed well in the qualifying tournament for Euro 2012 and beat Estonia 5-1 in another playoff to make the finals proper. With a backbone of goalkeeper Shay Given, defenders Richard Dunne and John O'Shea, Damien Duff in the midfield and the prolific Robbie Keane up front, the side was expected to cause the odd upset in the tournament.

Although the side hasn't graced many final tournaments over the years, it is almost universally agreed that the World Cups and European Championships that have the Republic of Ireland competing are of a higher quality, and their fans are among the liveliest and best-behaved of all international supporters.

The Czech Republic

Although the side is now known as the Czech Republic, it has competed under Czechoslovakia, Bohemia and Austro-Hungary. The national team was founded in 1901 and played its first competitive match (as Bohemia) in 1903. Over the next five years the side played against Hungary and England. By 1920, the team had become known as Czechoslovakia but it wasn't until the 1934 World Cup in Italy that they tasted international success.

A strong team was drawn against Romania in the first round but they dispatched them 2-1 to set up a quarter-final against Switzerland in Turin. The Czechs squeezed through 3-2 to meet archrivals Germany in the semi-final in Rome. An Oldřich Nejedlý hat-trick saw off their neighbours and guaranteed the Czechs a place in the final against the hosts. The match went to extra time but Italy eventually won 2-1. Much of the same team reached the quarter-final four years later but their next run in a tournament wouldn't come until the inaugural European Championships in 1960.

Although they lost to the Republic of Ireland in their first match, they then thrashed them 4-0 in Bratislava to set up a home and away tie against Denmark. They drew the first match but then hammered the Danes 5-1 to ensure a quarter-final against Romania, which they duly won 5-0 on aggregate. They lost the semi-final against the Soviet Union but beat France in a playoff to finish third in the tournament.

In the 1962 World Cup in Chile a strong Czech team beat Spain and drew with Brazil to reach the quarter-final. There they beat Hungary 1-0 before dispatching Yugoslavia 3-1 in the semi-final to guarantee a place against Brazil in the final. This time Brazil were too strong and they ran out 3-1 winners in front of seventy thousand fans in the Estadio Nacional in Santiago.

The side then failed to qualify for the next three European Championships and only made the first round of the 1970 World Cup in Mexico, but their fortunes were about to change. Czechoslovakia came through a difficult qualifying tournament for the 1976 European Championships in Yugoslavia where they met the Netherlands in the semi-final. Anton Ondruš opened the scoring for the Czechs but he then scored an own goal late in the second half and the match went to extra time. Two goals in the dying moments saw them through to a final against their neighbours and old rivals West Germany, the current World and European Champions.

Czechoslovakia went 2-0 up but the Germans fought back to take the final in Belgrade to extra time. There were no more goals so he match went to a penalty shootout, which the Czechs eventually won after Uli Hoeneß missed and Antonín Panenka scored a delightful chip. Because of the cheek and daring involved in choosing to chip the goalkeeper, his penalty is perhaps the most famous spot-kick ever scored.

The side didn't qualify for the 1978 World Cup, but 1980 brought renewed hope with a solid performance at the European Championships. They beat Greece and drew with the Netherlands to progress from their pool to the third/fourth playoff match, where they beat the hosts after an epic penalty shootout to finish third in the tournament. Later in the year the side won gold at the Moscow Olympics. Poor performances for most of the next decade saw them fail to qualify or be eliminated early from all the major championships until Italia '90 however.

The Czechs hammered the USA 5-1 in their opening match and then beat Austria before losing to Italy in their final group game. They finished second to the hosts in the pool and progressed to a knockout match against Costa Rica, which they duly won 4-1 to guarantee a quarter-final against the old enemy. This time West Germany were too strong but it had been a successful tournament for the Czechs. The country eventually dissolved into the Czech Republic and Slovakia in 1992, both of which were soon recognized by FIFA as separate football entities.

The republic's competitive debut came during the qualifying tournament for Euro '96. The side notched up six wins and finished top of their group above the favourites, the Netherlands. They then lost their first match in the finals against West Germany, but they recovered to beat a strong Italy and draw against Russia. Having finished second in their pool, they went on to beat Portugal at Villa Park and France on penalties at Old Trafford in the semi-final. The final was a rematch against the Germans but a Golden Goal from Oliver Bierhoff snatched victory for their archrivals.

Petr Cech keeps another clean sheet in training

The side then inexplicably failed to qualify for France '98 and, even more surprisingly given that they'd won all ten of their qualifying matches, were then dumped out of Euro 2000 at the group stage. Euro 2004 saw them return to form and they won all three of their pool matches against strong opposition (Latvia, the Netherlands and Germany). The side then dismantled the Danes to set up what looked to be a relatively easy match against the un-fancied Greeks. The match went to extra time, however, and Greece eventually won.

The Czechs started well at the 2006 World Cup but then lost two matches and failed to make it through their group. They also looked to be cruising to the knockout stages of the 2008 European Championships but, having been 2-0 up, three late goals from Turkey saw them eliminated. The side then failed to qualify for the 2010 World Cup. Pride was restored in November 2011 when they won a playoff against Montenegro to reach Euro 2012, however.

Croatia

Football came to Croatia with the British in 1873, and by 1907 several local clubs had been founded. A fledgling national team played against a provincial side that year but the bulk of the nation's players were recruited by the Kingdom of Yugoslavia before Croatian independence. In 1940 Jozo Jakopić led a representative side in the first of five unofficial friendly matches, while a further

The first Croatian team in 1940

fourteen FIFA-endorsed games were played before the end of the Second World War. As the state of Croatia ceased to exist after the conflict, the team was incorporated into the Republic of Yugoslavia, which was how things stood until 1990.

Before the declaration of independence in 1991, two teams still existed: Yugoslavia, which fielded several Croatian players, and Croatia itself, which, although still considered part of Yugoslavia, was a distinctly separate entity. Their first official match was played against Estonia in 1994 and resulted in a 2-0 victory. They promptly announced their arrival on the international stage by finishing top of their qualification group for Euro '96.

Having made it to the finals, the side beat Turkey and defending champions Denmark. Although they then lost to Portugal, they made it through to the knockout stages where they were beaten by Germany. Striker Davor Šuker was an inspiration at the tournament and he scored vital goals in the qualifying rounds for France '98. Although they were not expected to perform well at the World Cup, Croatia beat Jamaica and Japan and progressed from a tough pool to face Romania.

Croatia won the match 1-0 to confirm a quarter-final berth against the mighty Germans, then ranked second in the world. They avenged their Euro '96 defeat with an emphatic 3-0 victory but then lost 2-1 to eventual champions France in the semi-final. They raised themselves from the agony of defeat to beat the Dutch in the soul-destroying third/fourth playoff match. With six goals, Davor Šuker was the tournament's top scorer. His team completed a memorable year by moving into third place in the World Rankings, an astonishing achievement for a side so new to international football.

Sadly they were not able to continue this run of form and after two tense and politically charged matches against Yugoslavia they finished third in their qualifying group for Euro 2000 and failed to make it to the finals. Under new coach Mirko Jozić the side qualified strongly for the 2002 World Cup in the Far East but, despite beating Italy, losses to Mexico and Ecuador saw them eliminated at the group stage. They fell at the same stage during Euro 2004 having drawn with France and lost to England.

The 2006 World Cup should have been a high point after the side marched through the qualification tournament without losing a game, but they were defeated by Brazil in their opening match and could only manage a goal-less draw against Japan. Victory over Australia in their final group game would have given them hope but referee Graham Poll lost control and issued three yellow cards to Josip Šimunić before finally sending him off (Brett Emerton and Dario Šimić had already been dismissed for second bookings). The match ended in a 2-2 draw and Croatia were eliminated.

The side topped its qualification group for Euro 2008 by beating England home and away and only losing one game. They were strong again in the pool stage at the finals themselves and beat Austria 1-0, an excellent Germany 2-1 and Poland 1-0 in their final match. After a hundred and nineteen goal-less minutes against Turkey in the quarter-final, Ivan Klasnić thought he'd scored the winner but Semih Şentürk equalised in the dying moments to send the game to a penalty shootout, which the Turks then won.

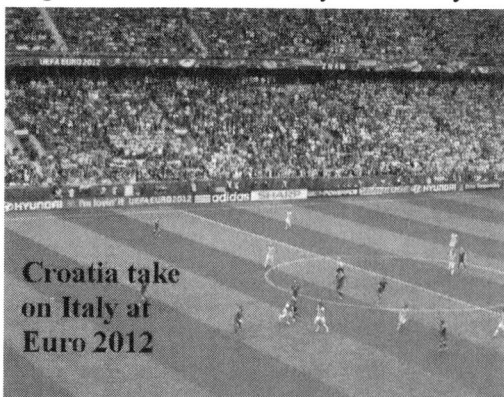

Croatia take
on Italy at
Euro 2012

Slaven Bilić remained at the helm for the qualification tournament for the 2010 World Cup in South Africa but humiliating losses to England as well as two draws saw them finish behind the English and the Ukraine. Although Bilić was again expected to stand down as head coach, he stayed for the Euro 2012 qualifying campaign. Despite surprise losses to Israel and Malta, the side eventually qualified for the tournament after beating Turkey 3-0 on aggregate in a playoff.

A friendly against Australia in late 2011 gave Bilić the chance to test a few younger players but he then announced he would be stepping down from the managerial post after the tournament.

Portugal

The Portuguese Football Federation was formed on the eve of the First World War so the national side didn't get to play a game until 1921, which ended in a 3-1 defeat to neighbours Spain. Over the next seven years the team played a series of friendly matches before being invited to the 1928 Olympics in Amsterdam. They made the quarter-final after solid performances against Chile and Yugoslavia but they were eventually beaten by Egypt.

Their first attempts to qualify for the World Cup were disappointing, a situation that didn't improve after the Second World War when they were humiliated 7-3 by Spain before the 1950 tournament and 9-1 by Austria before the following event. They failed again in 1958 and, despite a qualifying win over East Germany, they were then beaten by Yugoslavia and couldn't reach the last stages of the first European Championships two years later.

Eusebio is immortalised on a stamp

But the national team's stock was on the rise and, when the country unearthed a genuine superstar in Eusébio, their fortunes changed. They narrowly missed out on qualifying for the 1962 World Cup having drawn with England and beaten Luxemburg. They then targeted the European Championships but lost to Bulgaria after a replay. In 1966 the national side finally realised its potential. The team topped a difficult qualification group, which included Czechoslovakia,

57

Turkey and Romania, and then brushed the other teams in their pool aside with comparative ease, no mean feat when considering their opponents were Bulgaria (3-0), Hungary (3-1) and defending champions Brazil (3-1).

Star man Eusébio had already made a name for himself with vital goals and his glorious attacking runs but it was against the North Koreans in the quarter-final that he announced himself to the world as a serious challenger to Pelé as the greatest footballer. The Koreans took a surprise three goal lead but Eusébio scored four goals and Portugal eventually squeezed home 5-3. Although the side was then beaten 2-1 by hosts and eventual champions England, they won the playoff against the Soviet Union to finish third, and Eusébio ended the tournament as top scorer with nine goals.

With Eusébio becoming more of a peripheral figure, the national team's fortunes spiralled into decline and the next tournament they reached was the Brazilian Independence Cup in 1972. They recorded memorable victories over Ecuador, Chile, Iran, the Republic of Ireland, Argentina and the Soviet Union but lost in the final to a last-minute winner from Brazilian Jairzinho. Success at the World Cup or European Championships continued to elude the side however, and they didn't qualify for a tournament until Euro '84 in France.

The side drew against West Germany and Spain but secured their progress to the knockout stage with a 1-0 win over Romania in their final group game. The semi-final against the hosts was one of the greatest international matches in the history of the tournament. France took an early lead but Portugal equalised late on and sent the game into extra time. Rui Jordão scored his second to give Portugal the advantage with only a few minutes left on the clock but Jean-François Domergue then got his second. The match looked to be heading for penalties when Platini scored a last-minute winner to see the hosts through to a final against the Spanish.

Portugal recovered from the defeat to qualify from a tough group including West Germany, Sweden and Czechoslovakia for the World Cup in Mexico in 1986 but, although they beat England, they lost their next two games and were eliminated at the group stage. The side then failed to qualify for Euro '88 or Italia '90, and they also missed out on Euro '92 and the World Cup in 1994. However, they did claim their first senior trophy at an invitational tournament against Canada and Denmark in Toronto.

A new generation of players finally came good at Euro '96.

Portugal topped their qualification group and then beat Turkey and Croatia to reach the quarter-final, where they lost to the Czech Republic. France '98 was a disappointment but Euro 2000 saw their stock continuing to rise. Despite being 2-0 down against England in their opening match, they recovered magnificently and won 3-2. They then beat Romania 1-0 and the mighty Germans 3-0 after a Sérgio Conceição hat-trick. Two Nuno Gomes goals saw them past Turkey in the quarter-final but they eventually came unstuck against the French in the semi after Zidane scored a golden goal in extra time.

Qualifying for the 2002 World Cup went well and Portugal topped their group but the tournament itself was a shambles and they were eliminated after finishing third in their pool. They were chosen to host Euro 2004 and were one of the favourites for the title. They started poorly against Greece but recovered to beat Russia and Spain, and they then sent England out on penalties. Having beaten the Dutch in the semi-final they met the Greeks again in the final, but they lost again in a huge upset.

This strong side qualified comfortably for the 2006 World Cup and breezed through their group with wins over Angola, Iran and Mexico. In a bad-tempered match against the Dutch in which the referee brandished sixteen yellow and four red cards, the Portuguese scraped through 1-0. They again knocked England out on

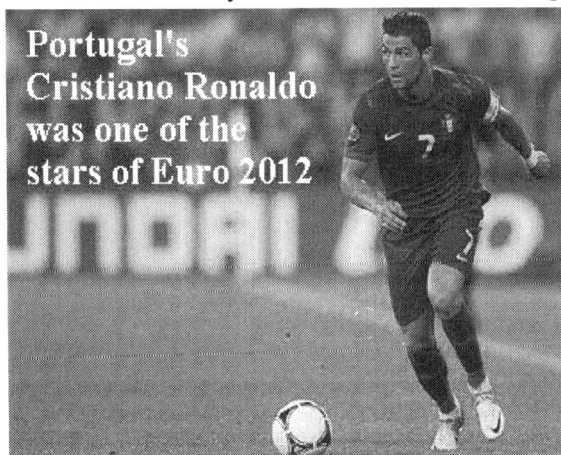

Portugal's Cristiano Ronaldo was one of the stars of Euro 2012

penalties in the next round before losing to France in the semi-final.

The side finished second in its qualification group for Euro 2008 but made it through a tough pool after victories over Turkey and the Czech Republic. The team then faced Germany in the quarter-final and lost 3-2. They squeezed through the qualifying campaign for the World Cup in South Africa but progressed to the knockout stages after draws with the Ivory Coast and Brazil and a comfortable 7-0 win over North Korea. They then faced the in-form Spanish in the round of sixteen and were eliminated 1-0.

A strong team featuring the likes of Cristiano Ronaldo, Raul Meireles, Nani and Nuno Gomes qualified for Euro 2012 after finishing second in their group behind Denmark but they then won a two-legged playoff against Bosnia & Herzegovina 6-2.

Germany

The German Football Association was formed in 1900 and it became the governing body for the national team in 1908. Their first match was in Basle against Switzerland in April of that year but they continued a trend set by a national select team that had played against England several times before the football association came into existence in that they lost comfortably. The players were chosen by the association until the appointment of the first dedicated coach, school teacher Otto Nerz, in 1923.

The financial hardship of the Great Depression in the early 1930s meant that the team couldn't afford to travel to the first World Cup in Uruguay but they showed well in the 1934 tournament in Italy and finished third. The 1938 event in France was less successful. The country was viewed with suspicion after Hitler had incorporated Austria into the empire. The talented Austrian team was promptly disbanded even though it had qualified for the World Cup. Some of their players were then forced to join a 'united' German side but they were immediately knocked out by the Swiss.

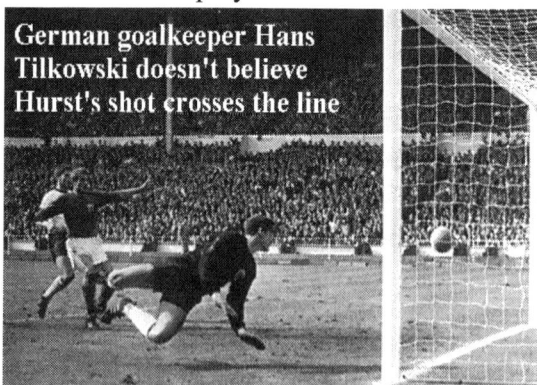

German goalkeeper Hans Tilkowski doesn't believe Hurst's shot crosses the line

Germany was divided after WWII but the new West German team soon qualified for the 1954 World Cup. They were trounced by the Mighty Magyars (8-3) in the first round but better performances saw them meet the Hungarians again in the final. This time coach Sepp Herberger fielded his strongest team against a side that had not lost for thirty-two games. In what has become known the 'Miracle of Bern' Germany came from two goals behind to win.

The West Germans again showed strongly in 1958, finishing fourth, although in Chile in 1962 they only reached the quarter-final. Realising they needed to make changes, the game was declared fully professional and a new Bundesliga was formed. The project worked and West Germany reached the final in England four years later, although they were beaten by a dubious Geoff Hurst goal. This ushered in a period of total dominance for the Germans, however.

The side avenged the 1966 defeat to England in Mexico before falling 4-3 to Italy after a thrilling semi-final, dubbed the 'Game of the Century', during which the inspirational Franz Beckenbauer played on with a dislocated shoulder. In their first appearance at the European Championships, Beckenbauer, now captain, guided them to the title with a comfortable 3-0 victory over the Soviet Union in the final at Euro '72. They repeated this success on home soil at the 1974 World Cup, although, having already qualified for the second phase of the tournament, they lost to archrivals East Germany.

They made a few positional and tactical adjustments for the final against the Netherlands but they were a goal down before a single German player had touched the ball. Their mental strength and physical fitness held firm under pressure, however, and they fought back to win 2-1 with goals from Paul Breitner and the outstanding Gerd Müller. Euro '76 saw West Germany appear in yet another final, although they eventually lost the penalty shootout against Czechoslovakia.

After a poor showing at the 1978 World Cup in Argentina, new coach Jupp Derwall guided the side to 1980 European Championships in Italy. They beat the Czechs and the Dutch, and drew with Greece to book a spot against Belgium in the final. A last-gasp Horst Hrubesch goal gave them the victory in front of forty-eight thousand fans in Rome's Olympic Stadium.

This golden age for West German football continued at the 1982 World Cup, when they reached the final again. Although they lost to Italy and underperformed in France at Euro '84, with Beckenbauer at the helm they reached the World Cup final in Mexico in 1986. This, however, was Maradona's tournament and the Germans were once again beaten finalists. Euro '88 on home soil handed them a painful lesson when they were beaten by their main enemy on the continent, the Dutch, in the semi-final.

The 1990 World Cup in Italy served up a rematch against

Maradona's Argentina in a negative final that the Germans won with a penalty late on. In so doing, Beckenbauer became the only man to captain and manage a team to victory in the World Cup final.

East Germany, on the other hand, couldn't match the success of their illustrious neighbours. Since the formation of a national squad in 1952, they only qualified for one World Cup (1974) and never made it to the finals of the European Championships. They enjoyed some success at the Olympics, however, taking bronze in 1964 and 1972, gold in 1976 and silver in Moscow in 1980. The side withdrew from the qualification campaign for Euro '92 after it became clear that the country was about to be reunited.

Although Beckenbauer had stepped down, the new Germany entered the 1992 European Championships with high hopes. They were eventually beaten in the final by the surprise team of the tournament in Denmark. A couple of barren years followed and they showed poorly at USA '94. Two years later they were back to their winning ways at Euro '96 in England. They defeated the Czech Republic and Russia, before drawing with Italy to top their group. They then overcame Croatia in the quarter-final to set up a semi-final against the hosts. After an epic encounter which saw Stefan Kuntz cancel out Alan Shearer's early strike and both sides hit the woodwork, the Germans squeezed through on penalties to meet the Czechs again in the final. Olivier Bierhoff won the match with a Golden Goal five minutes into extra time.

Oliver Bierhoff scores the golden goal to win Euro '96

The 1998 World Cup and the European Championships in 2000 marked the end of German invincibility and they performed poorly at both tournaments. As a result, they were not expected to do well at the World Cup in 2002 but they battled through to the final only to lose to Brazil. They were eliminated early from Euro 2004 but finished third on home soil at the 2006 World Cup. Although the side made hard work of their opening matches at Euro 2008, they still made the final against the world champions. Spain eventually won 1-0, a score-line they repeated in the semi-final of the 2010 World Cup in South Africa.

Germany topped their qualification group for Euro 2012.

Italy

Along with Germany and Brazil, Italy can claim to be one of the world's top footballing nations. With four World Cups, a European Championship and Olympic Gold in the bank, the Azzurri have built on traditionally strong defence to become a dominant force in the game.

Italy had an auspicious start in international football when they demolished a strong French side 6-2 in Milan in 1910, but they had to wait until 1928 before they won anything tangible, a bronze medal at the Amsterdam Olympics. Italy didn't travel to the first World Cup in Uruguay two years later but they made an immediate impact on home soil in 1934, winning the tournament and then successfully defending it in Paris in 1938.

The post-war national team was tipped to win the 1950 World Cup when tragedy struck. The aircraft carrying the Torino team (ten of whom would have started for Italy) crashed and a hastily reassembled Italy couldn't make it past the tournament's first round. Despite AC Milan and Internazionale dominating domestic European football in the 1950s, the national team couldn't capitalise on their success and failed to qualify for the first European Championships in 1960. They were then knocked out early four years later and it wasn't until the 1966 World Cup in England that they made the headlines, albeit for the wrong reasons. The pre-tournament favourites were humiliated by the semi-professionals of North Korea and were dumped out of the event.

Italy bounced back quickly from this devastating defeat and they won Euro '68 after a coin toss had seen them beat the Soviet Union in the semi-final (the game had ended 0-0 but in the days before penalty shootouts this was the preferred method for deciding matches). They met Yugoslavia in the final but the first match ended in a 1-1 draw. Italy won the replay in Rome's Olympic Stadium two days later.

The World Cup in Mexico in 1970 saw the Italians play in the 'Game of the Century' against the West Germans in the semi-final, which they eventually won 4-3, and then come up short against the best international football team of all time in the final, the magnificent Brazilians of Pelé, Jairzinho, Tostão, Rivelino and Carlos Alberto. The side was beaten by Poland in 1974 but showed well by placing fourth at the World Cup in Argentina in 1978 and

Italy prepare to take on Argentina at the 1982 World Cup in Spain

Euro '80 on home soil two years later.

A match-fixing scandal before the 1982 World Cup in Spain saw the team arrive in disarray and with the other sides suspicious of their results in qualification. The scepticism was well founded and Italy scraped through their group after three lacklustre draws. In the second round, they silenced their critics with victories over Maradona's Argentina and champions-elect Brazil, and they then comfortably beat the Germans in the final. It was to be their last tournament win for a quarter of a century.

Italy failed to qualify for Euro '84, were eliminated early from Mexico '86 and lost to the Soviet Union in the semi-final at Euro '88. Much was expected of them when the World Cup came to Italy in 1990, however. They progressed to the semi-final comfortably without conceding a goal but were then knocked out on penalties by Argentina. They then beat England in the playoff to finish third. Despite this strong showing, they inexplicably failed to qualify for Euro '92 in Sweden, the poor run all the more curious because they then made it to the World Cup final against Brazil at USA '94. Star of the tournament Roberto Baggio missed his penalty in the shootout, however, and they lost.

Italy were eliminated in the group stages of Euro '96, and France then knocked them out in the quarter-final of the 1998 World Cup. They were on course to win Euro 2000 after beating the Netherlands in the semi-final and leading against France in the final until Sylvain Wiltord equalised in the fourth minute of injury time. David

Trezeguet then scored the Golden-Goal winner in the hundred and fourth minute to break Italian hearts. The 2002 World Cup was another disappointing tournament and the Italians were knocked out by co-hosts South Korea, and they couldn't make it past the group stages at Euro 2004.

History repeated itself at the 2006 World Cup in Germany. The Italian leagues had been rocked by match-fixing scandals (much as they had in the build-up to the 1982 tournament) and the national side was in turmoil. Italy topped their group with two wins and a draw, and they then sneaked past Australia with a controversial penalty **Italian fans celebrate their side beating France in the 2006 World Cup Final.** late on. They beat Ukraine in the quarter-final and Germany in the semi to set up a final against the in-form French. It was another controversial match that saw Zinedine Zidane sent off after an altercation with Marco Materazzi. It was 1-1 after extra time but the Italians scored all of their penalties and won the trophy.

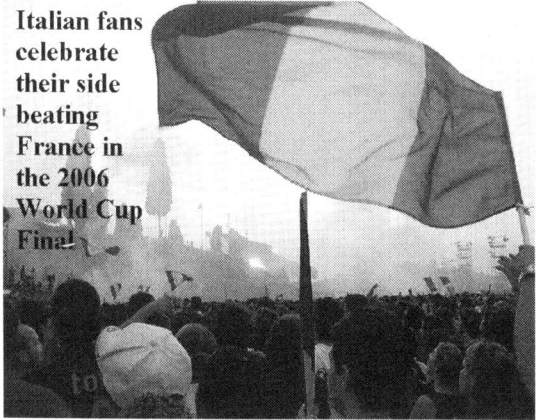

From the high of their World Cup triumph to the low of Euro 2008, which was a tournament to forget for the Azzurri. They lost their first match 0-3 to the Netherlands and only scraped through to the quarter-final, where they were beaten by eventual winners Spain. Although they travelled to the 2010 World Cup in South Africa with high hopes, the Italians could only draw against Paraguay and New Zealand before being humiliated by Slovakia. Having slumped into a trough, Italy bounced back strongly and comfortably topped their Euro 2012 qualification group.

Greece

Throughout its eighty-five-year history, the Greek national team has endured far more lows than highs. The Hellenic Football Association was formed in 1926 and became affiliated to FIFA the following year, and it was one of the founding members of the fledgling UEFA movement promoting European football in 1954. The association became the largest sports governing body in the country when it took control of the national league and international team immediately after its founding in the late 1920s.

Their first match, against Italy in 1929, resulted in a 4-1 hammering. They then spent decades in the international wilderness until they qualified for their first major tournament, the 1980 European Football Championships in Italy. It was a brief taste of the big time for them because they promptly lost to the Netherlands (1-0) and Czechoslovakia (3-1) before earning a creditable 0-0 draw against West Germany. They were eliminated having finished bottom of their group, however.

It took another fourteen years before they made it to the finals of the World Cup but USA '94 was equally miserable. They were thrashed 4-0 by both Argentina and Bulgaria, before losing their final group game to Nigeria (2-0). It emerged after their game with Argentina that Maradona had failed a drugs test and he was sent home in disgrace.

The team recovered well from this humiliating exit and only just missed out on qualification for Euro '96, a feat they would repeat during the qualifying campaign for the 1998 World Cup. Greece again finished their group in third place while trying to secure a place at Euro 2000. Their fortunes received an unexpected boost after a couple of disappointing defeats when they finished top of their qualifying group for Euro 2004 after an astonishing six straight wins at the end of the campaign.

In their opening match the Greeks surprised hosts Portugal, beating them 2-1 with goals from Giorgos Karagounis and a penalty from Angelos Basinas, and they then drew 1-1 against an in-form Spain, Angelos Charisteas cancelling out a Fernando Morientes strike. They were losing 2-0 to Russia in their last match and would have been eliminated were it not for a late Zisis Vryzas strike sending the Spanish home on goal difference. Their quarter-final against reigning champions France was equally memorable and they took the lead in the second half through Angelos Charisteas. Despite late French pressure, Greece held on to win, setting up a semi-final clash with the Czech Republic. It was the first time any team had beaten the hosts and the defending champions at the same tournament.

Having beaten the Netherlands, Denmark and Germany, the

Czechs were favourites to make the final but Greece held firm against wave after wave of attacks. After a goal-less match, Traianos Dellas scored a silver goal at the end of the first half of extra time and the Greeks joined Portugal in the final. Angelos Charisteas gave Greece the lead early in the second half and they held on to win 1-0 in what was later viewed as one of the biggest upsets in football history.

The country was expected to perform well on the back of this victory but they couldn't qualify for the 2006 World Cup. They soon turned this round, however, and made it to the Euro 2008 finals in Austria and Switzerland as winners of Group C. The tournament itself was a huge disappointment. They

Greece take on Spain in Salzburg during Euro 2008

were beaten by Sweden (2-0), Russia (1-0) and Spain (2-1) and, having finished at the bottom of their group, were eliminated with no points.

They finished second in their 2010 World Cup qualifying group and made it to the finals after a playoff victory over the Ukraine. Their opening fixture saw them lose to South Korea but they fought back to win against Nigeria in the next game. They were then eliminated by two late Argentine goals in their final pool match.

Qualification for Euro 2012 went smoothly and the Greeks remained unbeaten throughout the campaign, netting twenty-four points from a possible thirty despite them being in a tough group alongside Croatia and Israel.

The Netherlands

The national side falls under the jurisdiction of the Royal Dutch Football Association (KNVB), which selected its first team in 1905. Their best-known team was the total football outfit of Cruijff, Rep, Neeskens and Krol that dominated the game in the 1970s without ever winning the World Cup.

The national side played its first game against Belgium in the year of its formation. The match was tied at 1-1 after normal time but the Dutch scored three in extra time to claim a convincing victory. The team failed to perform well at the 1934 and 1938 World Cups and wouldn't make it to the finals again until 1974, by which time club sides Ajax and Feyenoord were pioneering the fluid passing and moving system for which Holland would become famous.

Under coach Rinus Michels the Dutch swept aside holders Brazil and then Argentina in the group stages before meeting archrivals Germany in the final. There was a lot of ill will between the sides as the Dutch still felt aggrieved by their treatment at the hands of occupying Nazi forces in the war and this was seen as a chance to right the wrong, on the sports field at least. The Dutch started well and earned a penalty before Germany had touched the ball. But the Germans were a resilient team and they fought back with goals from Paul Breitner and Gerd Müller. Despite late Dutch pressure, their neighbours held on to win.

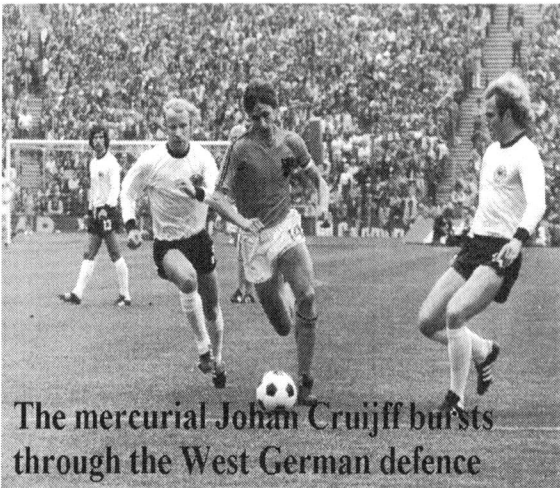

The mercurial Johan Cruijff bursts through the West German defence

Although much of the same team was predicted to do well at Euro '76, internal strife led to them taking their collective eyes off the ball and succumbing to eventual winners Czechoslovakia in the semi-final. Cruijff promptly retired but the Dutch still took a strong team to Argentina for the 1978 World Cup. They struggled in the first group stage but then drew with West Germany and beat Italy to set up a final against the hosts. The game looked to be heading for extra time when Rob Rensenbrink had a chance to win it at the death. He hit the post instead and Argentina scored twice in extra time to win the cup.

Dutch football slipped into decline with the retirement of the stars of the seventies and it wasn't until coach Rinus Michels was reinstated before Euro '88 that their fortunes were revived. Although they lost their first match to the Soviet Union, they qualified for the semi-final against the Germans with comfortable victories over England and the Republic of Ireland.

The semi-final between the old enemies was ill-tempered and challenges flew in from all angles, but Marco van Basten scored in the last minute to see them through to the final against their conquerors in the first match. Ruud Gullit and Van Basten made sure the Soviet Union couldn't repeat their earlier success and the Dutch claimed their first international trophy.

Despite having high hopes for Italia '90, the Dutch only scraped through the first round to set up yet another meeting against the hated Germans. It was another ugly game with two red cards that ended in a win for the Germans. Euro '92 also ended in disappointment as the side was eliminated after a penalty shootout against the tournament's surprise package, Denmark, in the semi-final. Euro '96 saw a promising young side (including the likes of Overmars, Cocu, Davids, Bergkamp, the de Boer brothers and Kluivert) soundly thrashed by England although they still made it through the group on goals scored before being eliminated by France.

Ruud Gullit in action for the Dutch

A resurgent side then made it to the semi-final of the 1998 World Cup, only losing to Brazil on penalties. The Netherlands co-hosted Euro 2000 with neighbours Belgium and they breezed through the opening round with three wins. They should have beaten ten-man Italy in the semi-final but couldn't convert two penalties in the match and another two in the shootout and they were eliminated.

The side failed to qualify for the 2002 World Cup in the Far East but they made it to the semi-final of Euro 2004 where they were beaten by Portugal. Coach Dick Advocaat was then replaced by former player Marco van Basten, the latter suddenly dropping many of the former stars before the 2006 World Cup campaign. They qualified comfortably for the latter stages but, in a game dubbed the

'Battle of Nuremberg' by the press because of the sixteen yellow and four red cards, they were again dumped out by Portugal.

They began Euro 2008 confidently, dispatching world champions Italy 3-0, then France 4-1 and Romania 2-0. Inexplicably, they then lost to Russia despite equalising in the last few minutes. A return to form saw them win all eight qualification games before the 2010 World Cup and they breezed through the opening rounds with wins over Denmark and Japan. They then overcame Slovakia and Brazil (both 2-0), before beating Uruguay for a place in the final against the Spanish. This was another ill-tempered match in which two Dutch players should have been sent off. They eventually lost 1-0. The Dutch carded nine wins from their ten qualifying matches for Euro 2012 and entered the tournament as one of the favourites.

Russia

The Soviet Union was formally established in late 1922 and the football team was founded nine months later. A representative side immediately beat Sweden in Stockholm but it wasn't until a 3-0 win over Turkey the following year that the side was recognised internationally. Strangely, this and the return fixture in Ankara were the only official matches played by the national team until the 1952 Helsinki Olympics, although a number of friendly games were organised in the interim.

Having won the gold medal at the 1956 Melbourne Games, the side entered its first World Cup in Sweden in 1958 with high hopes. They progressed from a tough group before knocking England out, although they were then beaten by the hosts in the quarter-final. Two years later they dominated the inaugural European Championship, beating Czechoslovakia in the semi-final and Yugoslavia in the final.

After a poor performance at the 1962 World Cup, the Soviets were keen to defend their European title. They beat Italy, Sweden and Denmark on the way to a final against hosts Spain but they eventually lost. They also performed well at the 1966 World Cup, earning a fourth-place finish after winning all their group games (against Italy, North Korea and Chile) but then losing to West Germany in the semi-final and Portugal in the playoff.

They made it to the finals of Euro '68 in Italy but their match against the hosts ended 0-0 and, as this was before replays for group matches and penalty shootouts, they were eliminated on the toss of a coin. They were then beaten in the playoff by England. Although they lost in the quarter-final of the 1970 World Cup, this heralded the end of a golden era for Russian football. Having made it to the final of the 1972 European Championships (where they lost to Germany), the rest of the decade was marred by disqualification from the 1974 World Cup (for refusing to play Chile) and failure to qualify for the European Championships in 1976 and 1980, or the 1978 World Cup. Despite this poor run of form, the Soviet Union won bronze medals at the next three Olympiads (1972, 1976 and 1980).

After poor showings at the 1982 and 1986 World Cups, the Soviets finally realised their potential at the 1988 European Championships in Germany, the last Euros they would contest as a unified team. Having beaten a strong Dutch side in their opening game, they went on to top their group. They then defeated Italy 2-0 to set up a return match against Holland in the final. This time the Dutch were too strong, Gullit's bullet header and Van Basten's volley winning the trophy for the 'Oranje'. The Soviet Union took some consolation by winning the gold medal at that summer's Olympics in Seoul.

They underperformed at Italia '90 but qualified well for Euro '92, although the break-up of the union meant that a hastily assembled CIS Team represented the country instead. The individual republics then declared their independence from Russia, although it was the new Russia that inherited the history and results of the former Soviet Union.

Having played their first international match against Mexico in 1992, Russia easily qualified for USA '94 but they couldn't make it past the group stage despite thrashing Cameroon 6-1. They also failed to make it into the knockout stages of Euro '96, and they couldn't qualify for either the 1998 World Cup or Euro 2000. Yet another poor performance followed as they were eliminated at the group stage of the 2002 World Cup. Euro 2004 yielded a similar result and they failed to qualify for the 2006 World Cup.

Under new manager Guus Hiddink, Russia performed well during the Euro 2008 qualifying tournament and progressed to the finals at England's expense. They were soundly beaten by Spain in their first match but recovered to beat Greece (1-0) and Sweden (2-0) to set up a quarter-final against pre-tournament favourites the

Netherlands. Roman Pavlyuchenko's early goal was cancelled out by a Ruud van Nistelrooy equaliser and the match went to extra time. Two late goals from Andrei Arshavin saw Russia through to their first major semi-final since the dissolution of the union. They met Spain in Vienna but were not good enough to trouble the champions-elect and eventually lost 3-0.

Hiddink then guided the Russians to the playoffs after a topsy-turvy qualifying campaign for the 2010 World Cup in South Africa.

Andrei Arshavin celebrates scoring against the Dutch in the semi-final of Euro 2008

They won the first leg against Slovenia at home, 2-1, but Slovenia's away goal would prove crucial in the second leg. Slovenia won it 1-0 and went through to the finals proper on the away goals rule. Hiddink stepped down as coach immediately afterwards.

New manager Dick Advocaat oversaw a strong qualifying campaign for Euro 2012 in Poland and the Ukraine. Russia topped their group with seven wins, two draws and only a single loss from their ten games.

Spain

Founded in 1909, the Royal Spanish Football Federation became a FIFA member four years later but they didn't play their first international until they beat Denmark 1-0 at the 1920 Olympic Games in Antwerp. Like so many European sides they didn't travel to South America for the first World Cup in 1930 but they performed well at the 1934 event in Italy, beating neighbours Portugal 11-1 on aggregate in the qualifying rounds and Brazil 3-1 in the finals themselves. They eventually lost to the hosts after a replay. This would be their last match with anything at stake until after the Civil War and re-entry to FIFA competitions in 1950.

They qualified for the 1950 World Cup and topped a group

including England, USA and Chile. This was the only World Cup to be decided by a round-robin format involving the group winners but Spain couldn't beat Brazil, Uruguay or Sweden and finished fourth, their best result for the next sixty years. The decade before the first European Championships in 1960 was marked by poor performances and although they qualified for the tournament they forfeited their place at the finals themselves because of political disagreements between Franco and the Soviet Union.

They qualified for the 1962 World Cup in Chile but couldn't progress from a difficult group including champions Brazil and Czechoslovakia. Spain then hosted the 1964 European Championships and they made it to the final with a 2-1 win over Hungary in the semi. Although the Soviet Union had also progressed to the final, this time Franco relented and the teams met in Madrid, the hosts running out 2-1 winners with goals from Pereda and Marcelino.

Despite having high hopes for the 1966 World Cup, Spain lost to West Germany and Argentina and couldn't make it past the group stage, and they then failed to qualify for all the major tournaments until the 1978 World Cup in Argentina. Although they drew with Brazil and beat Sweden, a loss to Austria eliminated them. Euro '80 was expanded to include eight teams but Spain and England couldn't make it through their group to the knockout stages.

Spain hosted the 1982 World Cup but they only managed to squeeze through their group after a 2-1 victory over Yugoslavia. They were then beaten by West Germany, with a draw against England effectively eliminating them. The qualifying tournament for Euro '84 saw a shift in their fortunes: they needed to beat Malta by eleven goals to secure a place at the finals instead of the Dutch but the 3-1 halftime score-line wasn't nearly enough. Spain notched nine goals in an incredible second half and topped the group.

They also topped their group at the finals proper after two draws and a good win against West Germany. They then overcame the Danes on penalties in the semi to set up a final with neighbours France. The match was finely poised when a Michel Platini free-kick squeezed under goalkeeper Luis Arconada's body and the French went on to win 2-0.

Spain once again topped their qualifying group before the 1986 World Cup but, despite four solid performances, they were eliminated after a penalty shootout against Belgium in the quarter-final. Euro '88 was a disappointment: Spain won their opening match but were then beaten by Italy and West Germany. They made it through to the knockout stages of Italia '90 but were eliminated by Yugoslavia. The side failed to qualify for Euro '92 but saved face by winning the gold medal at that year's Barcelona Olympics.

Under new coach Javier Clemente, Spain began a slow revival and gradually began to shake off their underachievers tag. They showed well at USA '94 but eventually lost to finalists Italy. They were also unlucky at Euro '96 when they had two goals wrongly disallowed for offside and a couple of good penalty shouts turned down in their quarter-final against hosts England. They eventually lost the match on penalties.

Although they were eliminated in the first round of France '98, there were signs that the side was still improving, and they ran champions France close at the quarter-final of Euro 2000. They then had another two goals disallowed in the quarter-final of the 2002 World Cup against South Korea and the hosts eventually won the shootout. Euro 2004 was a disappointment but they made it to the knockout stages of the 2006 World Cup.

Spain celebrate their third major trophy in a row

Coach Luis Aragonés then decided that if they couldn't out-muscle their opponents they would deny them the ball. This new tic-tac pass-and-move style, which evoked memories of the Dutch total football of the 1970s, saw them qualify comfortably and progress to the knockout stages of Euro 2008. Spain beat Italy on penalties in the quarter-final, Russia in the semi-final (3-0) and Germany in the final (1-0). Spain scored more goals than any other team (12), had the individual top scorer in David Villa (4) and contributed nine players to the team of the tournament. They had at last delivered on promise shown fifteen years earlier.

The 2010 World Cup in South Africa confirmed their status as the best team in the world. Now under the guidance of Vicente del Bosque, they went on a thirty-five-match unbeaten run that included a record fifteen consecutive wins. They were surprisingly beaten in their first match against the Swiss but they recovered to card wins against Honduras, Chile, Portugal and Paraguay. They then defeated Germany in the semi-final before seeing off the brutal Dutch in the final. They then qualified comfortably for Euro 2012.

England

The oldest national team in the world was founded in 1872 and the side played its (and the world's) first international match against neighbours Scotland later the same year (a representative match between the sides had been played two years earlier but it was not deemed a full international). They joined FIFA in 1906 and played their first matches on the continent two years later.

The Football Association and FIFA then fell out so England did not take part in any World Cup until their reintegration after the Second World War. A strong team travelled to Brazil for the 1950 tournament but, despite being one of the favourites, they were beaten by the complete amateurs of the USA in one of the biggest sporting upsets of all time. This football lesson was repeated when Hungary demolished England at Wembley (6-3) before completely humiliating them in Budapest (7-1). England and its players had suddenly been exposed and were not yet the World Champions-in-waiting they purported to be.

The FA realised something had to be done and a more professional England reached the quarter-final of the 1954 World Cup. The next tournament was another disappointment, however, as England drew all of their group games and were eliminated. The side failed to qualify for the inaugural European Championships two years later, but at the 1962 World Cup in Chile they sneaked through their group on goal average before losing to Brazil in the quarter-final. They then failed to make it to the 1964 European Championships.

The team finally came good on home soil at the next World Cup. After a nervy start against Uruguay, they beat Mexico and France to reach the knockout stages. The quarter-final against Argentina was an ill-tempered affair but England squeezed past the South Americans to meet Portugal. A 2-1 win saw them through to the final against West Germany. The epic match was tied at 2-2 after ninety minutes but England scored two (dubious if you're German) goals in extra time and won the Jules Rimet trophy.

Much of the same team helped them qualify strongly for Euro '68 in Italy but they went out to Yugoslavia in the semi-final. Goals from Bobby Charlton and Geoff Hurst helped them to a 2-0 win over the Soviet Union in the playoff and they finished third. Their defence of the World Cup in Mexico got off to a good start. They narrowly lost to Brazil in an epic match before beating Romania and Czechoslovakia to book a place against West Germany in the quarter-final. In another incredible match, England took a 2-0 lead and looked to be cruising to victory but, with Bobby Charlton off, Beckenbauer changed the game and the Germans avenged their 1966 final defeat, winning 3-2 after extra time.

With hooliganism becoming a serious issue, the 1970s marked a low point for English football. They failed to qualify for Euro '76 or the World Cup in either 1974 or 1978, and they were eliminated at the group stages of Euro '80 after losing to Italy and finishing behind Belgium. And although they didn't lose a match in Spain '82, they were dumped out after two goal-less draws in a second group stage. They then failed to qualify for Euro '84.

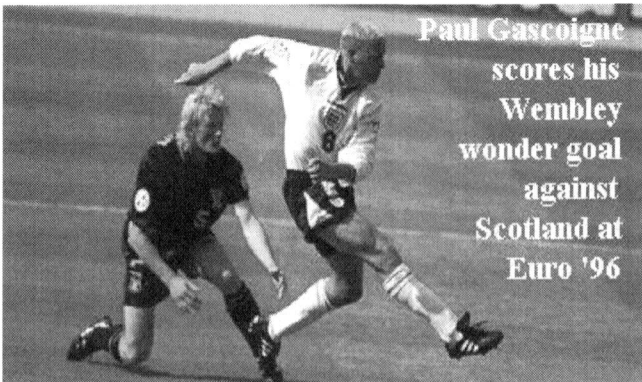

Paul Gascoigne scores his Wembley wonder goal against Scotland at Euro '96

The 1986 World Cup heralded an upturn in their fortunes, although it took a Lineker hat-trick to help them through the group stage. They then comfortably beat Paraguay to book a quarter-final spot against Argentina. In a game that had everything – great goals, close calls and the worst moment of cheating in football history – England were eventually eliminated at the hands of Maradona.

Euro '88 was an unmitigated disaster in that England lost all of their group games but, thankfully, Bobby Robson remained at the helm for the 1990 World Cup. England made hard work of their group but then dispatched Belgium and Cameroon to set up a semi-final against West Germany. In another close game, both sides hit the woodwork but the Germans eventually won the penalty shootout after the match finished 1-1.

The next two tournaments were entirely forgettable for England. At Euro '92 they didn't win a game, and they failed to qualify for USA '94. As hosts of Euro '96 they avoided the torture of qualification and didn't disappoint in the event itself. They drew with Switzerland before beating Scotland and hammering the Dutch to top their group. They were lucky to squeeze past Spain in the quarter-final before succumbing once more to the Germans in a shootout in the semi-final at Wembley.

With Glen Hoddle as manager and a strong team behind him, England were expected to do well at France '98, but they came unstuck against a belligerent Argentina in the second phase. And although they beat Germany in the group stage of Euro 2000, some terrible defending saw them eliminated after conceding three goals to both Portugal and Romania. England then edged out Argentina in the group stage at the 2002 World Cup in the Far East but, in what was to become a familiar story in subsequent tournaments, they were eliminated by Brazil in the quarter-final having taken the lead.

England take on Germany at the new Wembley

Despite taking the lead and then losing against France in Euro 2004, England still qualified for a quarter-final against Portugal, where they once again went ahead, then proceeded to play negatively and lost. They seemed to have recovered by the World Cup in 2006 and finished top of their group, but they crashed out on penalties yet again. Under new manager Steve McClaren, they failed to qualify for Euro 2008.

Fabio Capello oversaw a strong qualifying campaign for the 2010 World Cup in South Africa but England were poor and only scraped into the knockout stages where they were torn apart by a ruthless Germany. Another excellent qualifying series for Euro 2012 saw them stay unbeaten and top their group, but England traditionally under-perform when much is expected of them.

Sweden

The Swedish Football Association was formed in the early years of the twentieth century, and the national side's first fixture was against Norway in July 1908. A comfortable 11-3 win was followed by five heavy losses to stronger European opposition. In that year's London Olympics the side suffered another humiliating defeat to Great Britain, 12-1.

For the next twenty years Sweden only played friendly internationals, although they did manage bronze at the 1924 Olympics in Paris. They made their first World Cup appearance in Italy in 1934. They beat Argentina in the first round but then lost to Germany in the quarter-final. The next event was more successful and they eventually came fourth after losing to Hungary in the semi-final and Brazil in the playoff.

Their first tournament success came at the 1948 London Olympics. They beat Austria, Korea and archrivals Denmark to

The Swedes were runners-up at the 1958 World Cup

reach the final against Yugoslavia at Wembley, a match they won 3-1. It marked the beginning of a decade of good fortune for the national side. They qualified for the final group stage at the 1950 World Cup in Brazil and eventually finished third. They then hosted the 1958 event, easily progressing to the knockout stages after wins over Hungary and Mexico. They beat the Soviet Union and West Germany to reach the final against the Brazil of Garrincha, Pelé and Vavá, but they were soundly beaten 5-2.

If the 1950s had marked a high point for Swedish football, the following decade was littered with failure to qualify for the major championships. They lost a playoff against Switzerland to decide which team would go to the 1962 World Cup, failed to qualify for any of the European Championships (their first appearance would come in 1992), and only just made it to the World Cup in Mexico in 1970. The 1974 tournament saw an improved side ease through its group but they then lost to Poland and hosts West Germany to finish fifth. They qualified again for the 1978 event but finished bottom of their group.

Qualification for every World Cup in the 1970s was seen as a success, although the 1980s saw the side slump into another trough. They couldn't make it to any major tournament in the decade but did manage to redeem themselves by landing a place at Italia '90. Three defeats in the group stage saw them eliminated however.

There was cause for optimism two years later as Sweden hosted the European Championships for the first time. They advanced to the semi-final as group winners ahead of England, France and eventual champions Denmark, but they were then knocked out by Germany (3-2). This remains their best result at the tournament. The following World Cup in the United States confirmed their place at the top of European football. In the group stage they drew against Cameroon and Brazil, and beat Russia to reach the knockout stages. There they saw off Saudi Arabia and then Romania after a penalty shootout. In the semi-final they were beaten by a single goal from eventual champions Brazil. They secured third place with a comfortable victory over Bulgaria in the playoff.

Despite a superb qualifying tournament for Euro 2000 in which they only conceded a single goal and won every match except that against England at Wembley, the finals themselves were a huge disappointment: they lost to Belgium and Italy and could only manage a draw with Turkey and were dumped out at the first group stage. They found themselves alongside Argentina, Nigeria and England at the 2002 World Cup but they topped a difficult group and met Senegal in the knockout stages. Despite having numerous chances to win the game, Sweden were eliminated by a late Henri

Camara strike.

They entered Euro 2004 with low expectations but they thrashed Bulgaria 5-0 in their opening match and were suddenly viewed as one of the tournament favourites. They then drew with Italy and Denmark and qualified for the knockout stages. Their quarter-final against the Dutch was goal-less and they eventually lost the penalty shootout. They fell at the same stage, to hosts Germany, in the World Cup two years later.

Euro 2008 was a disappointment. Despite qualifying well and seeing off defending champions Greece in their first match at the finals, they then lost to Spain and Russia and were eliminated. It went from bad to worse with a disastrous qualifying campaign for the 2010 World Cup, although the national side bounced back and qualified for Euro 2012 with fine wins against Hungary, San Marino, Moldova, Finland and the Dutch.

Sweden line up during Euro 2012

Denmark

The Danish football team made an immediate impact on the world game by winning the gold medal at the Intercalated (unofficial) Olympic Games in Athens in 1906. They backed this up with a silver medal in London two years later and another silver in Stockholm in 1912. They were ranked the number one team in the world until 1920 but a gradual decline and lack of ambition from the Danish Football Association (DBU) saw them only play friendly matches outside of the traditional Nordic Championships. Indeed the side was excluded from the Olympics until 1948, which yielded a bronze medal.

The best footballers in Denmark were lured abroad to earn a living but the DBU refused to allow them to compete in the Olympics so Danish football slipped further behind the rest of

Europe. By 1960 they had started to show some improvement and they took silver at the Rome Olympics. Euro '64 was also a success. They progressed to the final tournament after wins over Malta, Albania and Luxemburg but they were then beaten by the Soviet Union and Hungary and eventually finished a creditable fourth.

The DBU finally abolished its amateur pretensions in 1971 in the hope that the national team would be revived and compete at subsequent World Cups and European Championships. Years in the wilderness had relegated the team to a lowly FIFA ranking, however, and it would take until 1982 before any tangible successes were achieved. Although the side failed to qualify for that year's World Cup, they did beat eventual champions Italy in their group. And so began the slow climb to European domination.

The Danish team that won silver at the 1912 Olympics

The side qualified for Euro '84 in France, but lost to the hosts in their first match. They recovered well to thrash Yugoslavia 5-0 before beating Belgium 3-2 to make it through to the semi-final against Spain. A close game that ended 1-1 was decided on penalties and the Danish were beaten 5-4. Denmark backed up this solid performance by qualifying for their first World Cup at Mexico '86. Despite performing strongly in their group, they were eventually eliminated in the second round by Spain.

Although much of the same side qualified for Euro '88, the tournament itself was disappointing. The Danes were narrowly beaten by Spain, Germany and Italy and they finished bottom of their group. They couldn't qualify for Italia '90 and looked like suffering the same fate for Euro '92 in Sweden when the side was handed a wildcard entry after Yugoslavia had to pull out (Civil War had broken out in the country and sanctions prohibited them sending a team to the finals).

The tournament started badly however. The Danes could only draw with England before losing to Sweden. But they were determined to make the most of their lucky break and secured a semi-final spot with a late win over France. They then knocked out defending champions Holland to book a place in the final against Germany, then world champions. Despite playing a negative brand of football throughout the tournament, they relied on stout defence and the unbeatable Peter Schmeichel in goal to stop the opposition scoring. They then hit teams on the counterattack and scored vital goals to secure a 2-0 win.

The Danes celebrate winning Euro '92

The 1990s saw the side endure several lows – such as failing to qualify for USA '94 – and enjoy a few highs – like beating Argentina 2-0 in the final of the 1995 Confederations Cup. They defended their European crown valiantly in 1996 with a win against Turkey and a draw with Portugal, but defeat to Croatia sent them home at the group stage.

Under the more offensive-minded coach Bo Johansson, the side qualified for the 1998 World Cup. They then beat Saudi Arabia and drew with South Africa to progress to the knockout stages. They thumped Nigeria 4-1 but eventually came unstuck against the mighty Brazilians (3-2) after a heroic performance. The side qualified for Euro 2000 but were poor in the tournament proper and Johansson resigned.

Under Morten Olsen they qualified for the 2001 World Cup and Euro 2004 but couldn't progress beyond the first knockout stage after heavy defeats by England and the Czech Republic respectively. They then failed to qualify for the 2006 World Cup or Euro 2008. And although the team made it to South Africa for the 2010 World Cup and beat Cameroon in their group, they were still eliminated after losses to the Netherlands and Japan. The side qualified strongly for Euro 2012, recording four wins, a draw and one defeat from their six matches.

3

The 2012 European Championships

The 2012 tournament was held in Poland and the Ukraine in June. (It was the last event contested by sixteen teams as, from Euro 2016 in France, the tournament will be expanded to include twenty-four nations.) Fifty-one nations entered the qualifying tournament. They were divided into nine groups, six of six teams and three of five. Although there were construction and infrastructure concerns in the lead-up to the tournament, UEFA President Michel Platini repeatedly visited the host countries to ensure they were keeping to their deadlines.

The tournament opened on June 8 with co-hosts Poland drawing 1-1 with Greece. Russia then demolished a strong Czech side 4-1 but the latter would recover and top their group after two victories. Poland drew against the Russians and lost to the Czechs and thus became one of the first sides to be eliminated. Despite finishing level on points with the Greeks, Russia also bowed out at the group stage.

Germany and Portugal went through from a strong Group B, with the former winning all three games. Denmark recorded a surprise 1-0 win over the much-fancied Dutch and the previous World Cup finalists ended up losing all their matches. Group C went to form, wit the Republic of Ireland and Croatia propping up the table. Spain and Italy drew in an entertaining opener and both went

through to the knockout stages. England continued their good form from the qualifying campaign and went through after drawing unconvincingly with France but then beating Sweden and co-hosts Ukraine. Despite losing their final game to the Swedes 2-0, France joined them in the knockout phase.

The first quarterfinal saw Portugal overcome the Czech Republic, a late Cristiano Ronaldo header sealing victory after a tense game in front of 55,600 fans in the national stadium in Warsaw. Ronaldo was living up to his billing as the finest player in Europe. This was his third goal in two games, and the second time in the tournament that he'd single-handedly won the match for his country.

Co-hosts Poland face Greece in the opening match of Euro 2012

The following day, Germany overpowered Greece in a thrilling match at the PGE Arena in Gdansk. The Germans took the lead just before the break through Philipp Lahm, but Giorgio Samaras equalised just after halftime. The Germans then eased clear with goals from Khedira, Klose and Reus before the Greeks pulled one back with a late penalty. For the Germans it was a world record fifteenth consecutive win; for the Greeks, an end to the tournament and their chances of repeating their shock win of eight years earlier.

Spain then took on the French at the Donbass Arena in front of 47,000 fans. For midfielder Xabi Alonso it was a memorable occasion: he scored both goals on his hundredth appearance for his country. France couldn't force Iker Casillas to make any notable saves and they bowed out of the tournament. They were the last team to eliminate Spain from a competition but that was back in 2006, and their southern neighbours have become a much stronger team in the intervening period.

The last quarterfinal saw England take on Italy at the Olympic Stadium in Kiev. More than 64,000 fans were treated to a high-intensity match played at a blistering pace, but it was Italy's imperious midfielder Andrea Pirlo who took control and was the tactical magician behind all their attacks. Although the Azzurri played with most of the possession, more creativity and seamless rhythm, they could not break England down and the match went to extra time. The half hour still couldn't separate them and the game had to be decided from the spot. Although Montolivo missed his, Ashley Young and then Ashley Cole also failed to convert and the Italians went through to the semi-final.

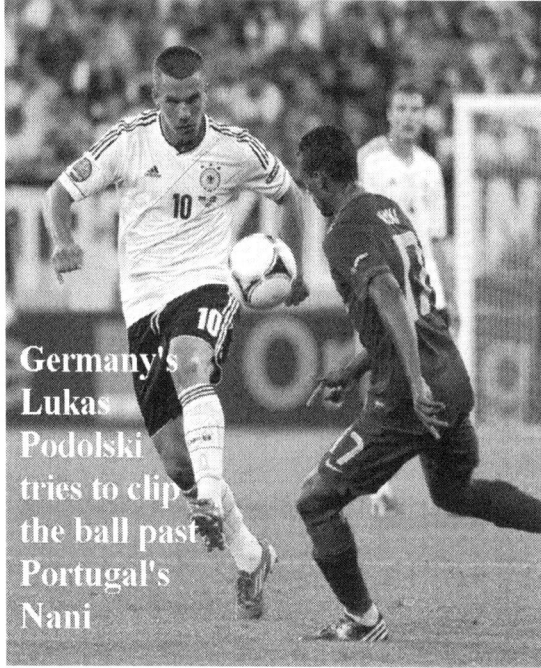

Germany's Lukas Podolski tries to clip the ball past Portugal's Nani

The first semi pitted the Spanish against archrivals Portugal. The game didn't live up to the hype and was a drab if tense affair that saw Ronaldo and the classy Spanish midfielders nullified by solid defensive displays. Indeed the Portuguese maestro, despite having several long-range pots at goal, only had one major chance to settle the match and that came in the last minute of normal time. Meireles broke through the Spanish defence and squared to Ronaldo but the striker sliced his shot high and wide and the teams entered extra time. Patricio denied Iniesta from close range, and the Portuguese 'keeper was in action again when he saved smartly from Navas. With no goals after 120 minutes, Patricio then saved Alonso's spot kick, but with Moutinho and Alves missing for their opponents, Spain went through 4-2.

In the second semi Italy faced the mighty Germans in Warsaw. It is perhaps one of football's quirks that Germany had never beaten Italy in seven previous competitive meetings and the Azzurri extended their winning streak to eight after Manchester City's controversial striker, Mario Balotelli, scored twice in the first half to set up a meeting with Spain in the final. Germany rallied in the second period but they could only manage a consolation Ozil goal from the spot in injury time.

The final in Kiev proved to be a step too far for the Italians and they were overwhelmed by some glorious attacking football from the Spanish. David Silva scored with a rare header early in the first half, and Jordi Alba scored an absolute peach as the half drew to a close. Hernandez and Iniesta continued to marshal the midfield after the break and the magnificent Pirlo was, for once, found wanting.

The poster advertising the final

The Spaniards' record against Italy was almost as bad as Germany's (they hadn't beaten the Azzurri competitively in nearly a century) but the third goal – from Torres after excellent work from Xavi – and another from Mata sealed a comfortable 4-0 win.

4

European greats, past and present

Patrick Vieira

The driving force behind Arsenal's resurgence in the mid-1990s, and a key player in France's World Cup and European Championship-winning squads in 1998 and 2000, Vieira has achieved just about every domestic and international honour.

He was born in Dakar in Senegal in June 1976 but his family moved to France in 1984. He immediately joined the youth team at FC Trappes, subsequently moving to FC Drouais and then Tours. He made his senior debut for Cannes in 1993 and a move to AC Milan followed two years later. After just a couple of appearances, the new Arsenal manager, Arsène Wenger, requested the player be transferred to North London, the deal eventually going through for just three and a half million pounds.

Vieira's height, stamina and overall ability allowed him to adapt to the pace of the English game relatively easily and he was soon launching attacks from midfield with his powerful runs and pinpoint passing. The side won the league and cup double in 1997/8 and he was immediately called up to the French national squad.

Vieira's grandfather had served in the French army so he was eligible to play for his adopted country and he made his international debut against the Dutch. He came on in the World Cup final in 1998 and provided the key pass that allowed Emmanuel Petit to score France's third goal. He was ever-present in

the European Championship-winning team two years later and he then took over the captaincy after Zidane's first international retirement in 2006. Although they reached that year's World Cup final, they were beaten by Italy. Vieira was injured for most of the Euro 2008 campaign and he officially retired when he was omitted from the squad that was humiliated in South Africa in 2010.

Domestically, Vieira was part of the double-winning Arsenal side in 2002, and he inherited the captain's armband after Tony Adams's retirement at the end of the season. In 2003/4 he led the side for its famous unbeaten season but a sixteen-million-pound bid from Juventus saw him move to Italy in 2005. The side won two league titles but, when they were stripped of both after the match-fixing scandal, Vieira moved to Internazionale and helped the Milanese to three Serie A titles. He rounded off his playing career with a move to Manchester City, where he promptly won the 2011 FA Cup. He now occupies a youth development post with the club.

Franco Baresi

Goalkeepers and defenders rarely attain the hero status afforded to strikers but Franco Baresi was an exceptional sweeper for AC Milan and marshalled one of the best defences in the game. His pinpoint tackling and overall ability on the ball made him one of the best defenders in the world for more than a decade.

Baresi was born in May 1960 in Travagliato in northern Italy. His parents died when he was in his teens so he looked for an outlet in football. Internazionale rejected him so he tried to join rivals AC Milan, eventually succeeding after his third trial at the age of fourteen. He soon established himself in the first team as Milan won the Scudetto (Serie A championship), and so began a lifelong association with the club. Baresi became known as the Steel Man, leading what many believe to be the best back four in the history of the game (alongside Paolo Maldini, Allesandro Costacurta and Mauro Tassotti).

The club was found guilty of match rigging in 1980, so they were fined and relegated to Serie B but Silvio Berlusconi stepped in, bringing in a relatively unknown manager, Arrigo Sacchi, while also spending money on transfers. With Baresi as captain, the team won the Italian league five times in the late 1980s and early 1990s; the

European Champions Cup in 1989, 1990 and 1994; as well as the Intercontinental Cup in 1989 and again in 1990. When he hung up his boots in 1997 after 716 games, the club retired the number six jersey in his honour.

Baresi came late to international football and he only made the bench during Italy's World Cup-winning run in Spain (1982). He made his debut against Romania later that year but refused to play while Bearzot was in charge which meant he missed the 1986 finals in Mexico. With Baresi at the centre of their defence, the Azzuri reached the semi-finals of the 1988 European Championships in West Germany before losing to the USSR. In the 1990 World Cup in his home county, Italy reached the semi-finals before losing to Argentina. They then beat England to finish third after a play-off.

Despite a slow start at the 1994 World Cup in the USA, Baresi captained his side for their cautious final against Brazil that ended 0-0. Baresi missed his penalty in the shoot-out and Roberto Baggio blasted his over the bar to hand victory to the South Americans.

After retiring, Baresi has stayed in the game that he graced. He now works as a talent scout and youth team coach at his beloved AC Milan.

Eric Cantona

Voted Manchester United's greatest player, 'King' Cantona was the key to the club's revival in the 1990s. He also enjoyed spells for several club sides in his native France and, although he didn't make the final team, he was the lynchpin of an improving national squad that went on to win the World Cup on home soil in 1998.

Cantona was born in Marseille in May 1966 and he soon took a liking to the sport of football. He joined local side SO Caillolais alongside Jean Tigana and Christophe Galtier as a goalkeeper but he was eventually persuaded to play up front for more than two hundred matches. It wasn't long before he was spotted by a big club and he joined Auxerre's youth team in 1981. He made his first-team debut two years later and consistently strong performances saw him called

up to the national squad, although his poor discipline often let him down.

After a number of high-profile bust-ups with fellow professionals, fans and coaches, and several loan spells during which he failed to control his temper, he announced his retirement aged only twenty-five. Gérard Houllier convinced him to rebuild his career in England, a move endorsed by French coach Michel Platini. Having helped Leeds to the league title in his first season, he moved to Manchester United. More success followed when United took the inaugural Premier League title, a trophy they retained the following season. They also won the FA Cup to complete an historic double.

Controversy stalked him throughout his career and it reared its ugly head again after he was sent off against Crystal Palace in 1995. As he walked off, he assaulted a fan with a karate kick and was banned for the remainder of the season. He was also stripped of the French captaincy. He was instrumental in helping United overhaul Newcastle in his comeback season, however, a year in which he became the first foreign player to lift the FA Cup as captain as United completed a second double. He retired from club football in

1997 at the age of thirty, a number of accolades – one of a hundred league legends, entry to the English Football Hall of Fame and Overseas Player of the Decade – doubtless convincing him that he'd made the right decision.

Cantona made his full international debut against West Germany in 1987 but he didn't get on with manager Henri Michel and he was dropped. Platini reinstated him but France performed poorly at Euro '92 and Platini was replaced by Gérard Houllier, the coach then handing Cantona the captain's armband for the qualifying matches before USA '94. France didn't make it to the finals and, despite Cantona getting the best out of the players and their vote, he was dropped after the Crystal Palace incident. New coach Aimé Jacquet left him, Jean-Pierre Papin and David Ginola out of the 1998 team, a decision that was initially seen as sacrilegious but one that was vindicated when France won the World Cup.

Cantona has now turned his considerable talents to the stage and screen, although he hasn't ruled out a return to football management, with Manchester United top of his wish-list of clubs. He recently took the first steps back into the game by taking over as Director of Football at New York Cosmos.

Ruud Gullit

One of the most versatile players to grace the game, Gullit was an inspirational captain who led the Netherlands to victory in the 1988 European Championships. He enjoyed success with the top clubs in Holland, Italy and England before turning his considerable talents to management.

Born Ruud Dil in a poor area of Amsterdam in September 1962, he played street football throughout his youth with the likes of Frank Rijkaard. He was soon picked up on the radar of team DWS and he then made it into the Dutch youth team alongside the Koeman brothers and Wim Kieft. As a precociously talented teenager he made his debut for HFC Haarlem and he was named the best player in the division. Several English clubs turned him down so he moved to Feyenoord in 1982 and ended up playing alongside the great Johan Cruijff. The following season the club secured the league and cup double and, having been named footballer of the year, he moved to domestic giants PSV, where he was also named the best player in his first season. A big-money move to AC Milan in 1987 brought more success: the Scudetto and two European Cups, but injuries forced him to watch from the sidelines for much of the early 1990s.

Such a talent was bound to make an impression on the international stage and Gullit didn't disappoint, although his early years were characterised by poor team performances. He made his debut aged nineteen in 1981 but the Netherlands repeatedly failed to qualify for the main tournaments and it wasn't until Gullit was captain that they qualified for the 1988 European Championships.

Although the Dutch lost their first match against the Soviet Union, they progressed by beating England, the Republic of Ireland and then Germany in a grudge match in Hamburg. The final was a re-match against the Russians but a close-range Gullit header and a magical Van Basten volley secured the trophy for the Dutch, their first international silverware. Although touted as potential champions of the world at Italia '90, Gullit's knee injuries and several underwhelming performances saw them lose to the Germans in another ill-tempered match in the second round. Euro '92 looked like being a strong tournament for the Dutch but they came unstuck against an inspired Denmark in the semi-final and went out on penalties. Frequent altercations with new national coach Dick Advocaat led to Gullit's retirement from international football in 1994.

He then moved to England, becoming one of the first international stars to grace the Premiership, and the likes of Gianfranco Zola, Dennis Bergkamp and Eric Cantona soon followed. Gullit seemed happiest in London and he took the playing managerial role at Chelsea when Glen Hoddle left to take the vacant England job. They finished sixth in the league and won the FA Cup. He then enjoyed spells at Newcastle, Feyenoord and Los Angeles Galaxy before taking up a punditry position with the media.

Didier Deschamps

A defensive midfielder with a superb touch, good pace and great tactical awareness, Deschamps will be forever remembered as the man who captained France to World Cup glory in 1998 and repeated the feat on the European stage two years later. It could all have been different, however, if he'd stuck to rugby in his youth.

Didier Claude Deschamps was born in Bayonne in October 1968. He was drawn to the oval ball game but was lured from Olympique Biarritz by amateur football side Aviron Bayonnais as a schoolboy. He was then spotted by scouts from Nantes in 1983 and he made his league debut two years later. He spent a couple of years with the club before transferring to Marseille and helping them to two league titles and the Champions League in 1993.

It was only a matter of time before the inspirational young captain was snapped up by one of the top clubs in Italy, Spain or England and Deschamps chose Juventus. He helped the side win an impressive tally of seven trophies in five years before moving to Chelsea, where he won the FA Cup in 2000. He then enjoyed a short spell in Spain with Valencia before hanging up his playing boots at the comparatively young age of thirty-two.

Although he could list a great many domestic triumphs on his CV, it was on the international stage that Deschamps became immortalised. He was given his first cap by Michel Platini in 1989 but France were a poor side in transition and they failed to qualify for the World Cup in 1990 and 1994. He was almost dropped from the side when Aimé Jacquet began rebuilding for the 1998 World Cup in France but he was one of the veterans who survived the chop while Cantona and Ginola did not.

As captain of a so-called Golden Generation that included the likes of Zinedine Zidane, Patrick Vieira and Thierry Henry,

Deschamps led the side to the semi-final of Euro '96. On home soil two years later, the French brushed aside all-comers and then defeated Brazil 3-0 in the World Cup final at the Stade de France. Euro 2000 was equally successful, France beating Italy with an extra-time Golden-Goal winner from David Trezeguet in the final in Rotterdam.

Having retired, Deschamps immediately took to management, guiding AS Monaco to their first appearance in the Champions League final. He then moved back to Juventus, a club in disarray after a match-fixing scandal had seen the side relegated to Serie B. Deschamps led them back into the top flight but resigned immediately afterwards citing difficulties with the club's board. Deschamps then oversaw Marseille's first league title in eighteen years. He is still with the club.

Alan Shearer

A prolific goal-scorer at club and international level, Shearer was the dominant English striker for more than a decade at the turn of the millennium. He briefly managed his beloved Newcastle and has recently been linked with a return to top-flight management but he continues to work as a pundit for the time being.

Shearer was born in Newcastle in 1970 and, like so many of the best players, he learned to play on the streets before starring for Gosforth School. He then joined amateur side Wallsend before being spotted by scouts. He had trials with a number of different clubs but was eventually signed by Southampton in 1986. He spent two years with the youth squad before making an impact in the first-team when he scored a hat-trick against Arsenal as a seventeen-year-old.

He performed consistently over the next few years and earned a call-up to the England squad for

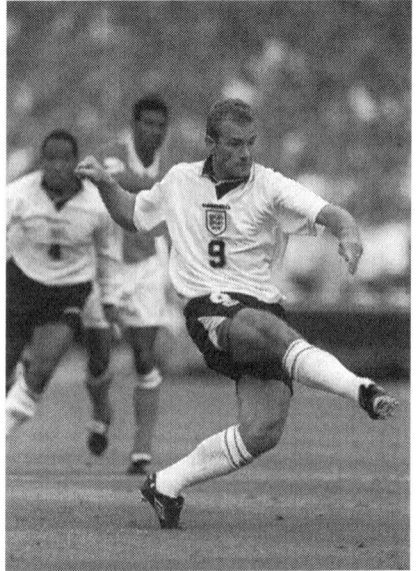

Euro '92 but the side were dumped out at the group stage. Shearer was now in demand and he moved to Blackburn that summer. He soon formed a strong partnership with Chris Sutton and Blackburn won the 1995 league title. His England outings were also yielding more goals. At Euro '96 on home turf, Shearer was unplayable and netted five times in England's run to the semi-final.

He was prolific once more in the build-up to the 1998 World Cup but England fell to Argentina after Beckham was sent off. He was on target again in the qualifying rounds of Euro 2000 but England again performed poorly and he retired from international football on a low note.

Domestically, however, he was enjoying his best years. He signed for his beloved Newcastle United for a world-record fifteen million pounds in 1996. For the next decade he terrorised defences with his strength and fearsome striking and in 2006 he finally broke Newcastle legend Jackie Milburn's goal-scoring record for the club when he notched for the two hundred and first time. Injuries then brought about his retirement.

At the end of the 2009 season, he was recruited to help Newcastle avoid relegation but he didn't have enough games and they duly fell into the Championship. Shearer now raises money for charity and works as a television pundit.

Laurent Blanc

In a playing career spanning more than twenty years, Blanc racked up over six hundred league appearances and a hundred and fifty goals, an impressive haul for a defender. He made ninety-seven starts for his country and was integral to the victorious World Cup and European Championship sides in 1998 and 2000. He now manages France.

Laurent Robert Blanc was born in November 1965 in Alès, France. He joined the Montpellier youth team in 1981 and graduated to the senior side as an offensive midfielder two years later. His eight years at the club yielded three hundred appearances and more than a hundred goals, and, having been persuaded to move into the defence, he was lured to Napoli for a season.

He returned to French outfit Nîmes the following year but moved again, to Saint-Étienne, in 1993. He then helped Auxerre to a league and cup double in 1995/6. After an unhappy year with Barcelona he moved to Marseille and then Internazionale, where he was voted club player of the year. He then moved again, this time to Manchester United. He was criticised for his first few performances but he was the rock in defence for the Premier League-winning campaign in 2002/3. He retired at the end of the season.

If his domestic footballing career was punctuated with highs and lows and regular moves, his international career was littered with success and relatively stable. He made his French debut in 1989 but the side failed to qualify for the 1990 World Cup. With Blanc at the heart of the side, however, the French then went on a nineteen-game unbeaten streak that saw them emerge as joint favourites for the 1992 European Championships. They were knocked out in the pool stages by eventual winners Denmark.

After another poor run of performances saw them fail to reach USA '94, Blanc announced his international retirement but new coach Aimé Jacquet convinced him otherwise and he became an integral part of the Euro '96 and 1998 World Cup squads. During the latter tournament, Blanc scored the first golden goal in the competition's history when the French knocked out Paraguay. Sadly for him, he missed the final after being sent of against Croatia in the semi-final. Despite being criticised for his age and lack of pace, he was solid throughout the victorious Euro 2000 campaign and he retired on a high at the end of the tournament.

Blanc moved into management in 2007 and he brought success to Bordeaux the following year when they won the league and cup double. In 2010 Blanc was named as the new manager of France. He guided them to the top of their group and qualification for Euro 2012.

Franz Beckenbauer

A true football legend, Der Kaiser won the World Cup as a player and manager. In his prime, he read the game better than anyone else and invented the attacking defensive sweeper's position. His precise passing, technical superiority and superb leadership made him the focal point for Bayern Munich and West Germany for nearly twenty years. As manager of the national team, he masterminded their World Cup victory at Italia '90.

Franz Anton Beckenbauer was born in 1945 in the ruins of post-war München (or Munich). He started playing football for youth side SC Munich 1906 aged only eight. After impressing at an under-14s tournament, he decided to join Munich's second club, Bayern, in 1959. Three years later he gave up his job and became a professional player. Bayern won promotion to the top flight in his first full season.

By 1968/69, Beckenbauer, now captain, led the team to its first championship in thirty-seven years. With him at the heart of the team, the goal-machine Gerd Müller up front and the excellent Sepp Maier between the sticks, Bayern dominated European club football throughout the early 1970s. In 1977, Beckenbauer stunned the world by signing for New York Cosmos in the North American League (along with Pelé) but he returned to Germany after four seasons.

Beckenbauer's international career was equally spectacular. In 1965 he earned the first of more than a hundred caps and he played every game in the 1966 World Cup in England, scoring four goals before having to man-mark Bobby Charlton in the final. West Germany avenged the defeat by the hosts four years later when they knocked England out in the quarter-finals of Mexico '70 after being

2-0 down. Beckenbauer broke his collarbone against Italy in the semi-final but played on, although his team eventually lost a thriller.

Beckenbauer then led Germany to victory in the 1972 European Championships in Belgium with a convincing 3-0 win over the USSR in the final. They backed this up with a superb display as hosts of the 1974 World Cup. Although they trailed to the mighty Dutch in the final, the Germans remained calm and fought back to win 2-1. They showed the same determination in the semi-final of 1976 European Championships in Yugoslavia where they came from 2-0 down to beat the hosts 4-2 in extra time, although they then lost to Czechoslovakia in the final.

Beckenbauer retired shortly afterwards but was soon convinced to take over as national team coach. He promptly guided an average team to the World Cup final in Mexico in 1986, although they lost 3-2 to Argentina. In the 1988 European Championships, old rivals the Netherlands knocked them out in the semi-finals but, two years later, Beckenbauer completed a remarkable double by managing the team that won the World Cup in Italy, the only man to win the trophy as a captain and a manager.

Still an influential figure in European football, Beckenbauer returned to manage Bayern Munich before becoming club president. He helped organise the bid for the 2006 World Cup in Germany.

David Villa

Nicknamed 'The Kid' on account of his youthful looks, Villa has broken just about every scoring record since he started playing with Sporting de Gijón. A big-money move to Barcelona and unparalleled success with the Spanish national side have confirmed his place at the peak of the world game alongside the likes of Argentina's Lionel Messi and Portugal's Cristiano Ronaldo.

David Villa Sánchez was born in December 1981 in northern Spain. Aged four he broke his right leg but his father managed the injury so well that by the time he recovered he could use both feet equally. Despite becoming disheartened at a lack of success in his teens, he joined the Mareo football school at seventeen. Sporting gave him his big break and he repaid them with forty goals in two seasons. He then moved to Real Zaragoza and his goals helped them win the Copa del Rey, which earned him a call-up to the national squad. A move to Valencia in 2005 was all the more noticeable because he made a habit of beating the giants of Barcelona and Real Madrid.

His first international tournament was the 2006 World Cup in Germany. He and fellow striker Fernando Torres guided Spain to the knockout stages but they were eventually beaten by France. The tone had been set for Spanish domination, however, and by the 2008 European Championships Villa and co were finally ready to realise their potential.

Although he was injured in the semi-final, Villa's goals brought him the Golden Boot and Spain the trophy, their first international silverware. He was on target again in the build-up to the 2010 World Cup in South Africa, scoring in several qualifying matches. The tournament itself began badly with defeat to Switzerland but it was a temporary blip and he was back to his best against Portugal and Paraguay. He was relatively quiet in the final against the brutal Dutch but Spain lifted the trophy and Villa was presented with the Silver Shoe and a place in the team of the tournament. He scored his record fiftieth international goal during Spain's impressive qualifying performances before the 2012 European Championships.

A move to Barcelona was somewhat inevitable given his precocious talent and he joined the Catalans for thirty-five million pounds in 2010. Along with superstars like Lionel Messi, he helped Barca become all-but invincible and they won La Liga and the Champions League in 2011. In September he broke his leg in a club match and missed most of the following season and the European Championships. If he can recapture his form of a couple of years ago, David Villa looks set to join the all-time greats of the sport.

Sir Bobby Charlton

Sir Bobby Charlton is an English sporting hero. A gifted attacking midfielder with a devastating shot, he survived the Munich air disaster and helped Manchester United to league and European Cup glory, as well as being England's goal-scoring playmaker in 1966.

Robert Charlton was born into a football-mad family in Northumberland in October 1937 (his uncle was Newcastle United legend Jackie Milburn) but it was his mother, Cissie, who coached Bobby and brother Jack in their youth. Bobby was seen playing for East Northumberland schoolboys by a Manchester United talent scout and representatives from eighteen clubs battled to secure his signature. At just fifteen, he signed for Manchester United, becoming one of the Busby Babes.

Charlton worked his way through the youth and reserve teams and eventually made his first-team debut in 1956. He scored twice and was soon holding down a regular place in the side that won the 1957 title. At Busby's insistence Manchester United entered the European Cup and were only narrowly defeated by the great Real Madrid side in the semi-final. The following season, United were returning home after their quarter-final victory against Red Star Belgrade when their plane crashed on take-off after a refuelling stop in Munich. Seven of Charlton's team-mates were killed instantly and Duncan Edwards died two weeks later. Despite the tragedy, United still competed well in the league and made it to the FA Cup final. At just twenty, Charlton was now the key to Busby's Manchester United rebuilding program.

He made his international debut against Scotland later that year and he was then named in the squad for the 1958 World Cup Finals in Sweden. He didn't play however, and England were eliminated in the group stages. The 1962 World Cup in Chile was also disappointing. Despite playing at the top of his game, Charlton couldn't lift his team to beat Brazil.

On the domestic front, the addition of Nobby Stiles, Dennis Law and George Best proved inspired and United won the league in 1965 and 1967, but the year in between was Charlton's annus mirabilis. He won the Football Writers' Player of the Year and European Footballer of the Year accolades, and he then guided English football to its peak when they won the World Cup. Franz Beckenbauer later reflected on the final against West Germany: "England beat us in 1966 because Bobby Charlton was just a bit better than me." The lynchpin of England's triumph, he was voted the best player in the tournament.

Further glory followed with the European Cup in 1968 as United became the first English team to lift the trophy. Charlton scored twice as United beat Portugal's Benfica 4-1 after extra time. Shortly afterwards, he also scored his forty-fifth international goal, breaking Jimmy Greaves's record. Later that year, England were knocked out of the European Championships in the semi-finals and both Bobby and Jack retired from international football after England's disappointing 1970 campaign in Mexico.

Charlton then founded several soccer coaching schools in the UK (where David Beckham was spotted), USA, Canada, Australia and China, before he became a director at Manchester United in 1984, a position he still holds. A true ambassador for English sport, Charlton was the driving force behind Manchester's Olympic bids in 1996 and 2000, as well as London's successful bid. As Sir Matt Busby once said, "He was as near perfection as a man and player as it is possible to be."

Cristiano Ronaldo

The most skilful and exciting player of the current generation, Cristiano Ronaldo is now a global footballing superstar. He uses either foot to dribble past defenders for Real Madrid and Portugal before accelerating and shooting past the world's best goalkeepers.

Cristiano Ronaldo dos Santos Aveiro was born in February 1985 in Funchal, Madeira. He often played against older boys and by the age of ten his exceptional talent was spotted by Sporting Lisbon. He was only twelve years old when he moved to the mainland to work his way through the youth teams. Aged seventeen, he scored twice on his first-team debut, and Manchester United's players convinced manager Sir Alex Ferguson to sign him in 2003. It was an inspired move and Ronaldo was soon lighting up the Premiership with his dazzling flair.

He earned his first Portuguese cap against Kazakhstan in 2003 and went on to become the star of the European Championships on his home soil in 2004. At the 2006 World Cup, the Portuguese were criticised for their unsporting behaviour, with Ronaldo becoming public enemy number one in England after he appeared to get club-mate Wayne Rooney sent off in their clash with England.

Sir Alex Ferguson convinced Ronaldo to stay at United and he and Rooney were soon terrorising defences while winning the league in 2006/07, a year in which he also won the PFA Fans' Player of the Year, the Football Writers' Association Footballer of the Year, Barclay's Player of the Season, PFA Young Player of the Year, and PFA Player's Player of the Year. He was named in the PFA Team of the Year, as well as being the Portuguese Footballer of the Year.

In 2009 he signed for Real Madrid for a world record eighty million pounds. In the 2010/11 season, he underlined his continuing maturity and devastating finishing by notching an incredible fifty-three goals. He and Argentina and Barcelona's maestro Lionel Messi are the only players to stand head and shoulders above their contemporaries in the game today. He continued to improve throughout the 2011/12 season and notched up his one hundred and fiftieth Real Madrid goal in only his hundred and forty-ninth appearance.

Johan Cruijff

The most gifted footballer of his generation, Johan Cruijff led the total football revolution with Ajax Amsterdam and the Netherlands in the 1970s. Blessed with exceptional skill, pinpoint passing and a terrific turn of speed, he became synonymous with the way the beautiful game should be played. He went on to lead Barcelona to domestic and European cup triumphs as a visionary manager in the early 1990s.

Hendrik Johannes Cruijff was born in April 1947 in a suburb of Amsterdam. He enjoyed football from a young age and by his tenth birthday he'd been picked from over two hundred children to join the Ajax youth team. Seven years later he was playing in Rinus Michels's revolutionary first team at Ajax Amsterdam that allowed the players to rotate positions in an adventurous and fluid style.

This suited Cruijff's style and he turned up all over the pitch and ran teams ragged. He made his debut against FC Groningen in 1964 and scored Ajax's only goal. After another 274 appearances, he'd scored a barely believable 204 goals in a period that Ajax were dominating both the Dutch league and Europe, where they took three consecutive European Cups.

In 1973 Cruijff followed Rinus Michel to Barcelona for a world record fee of nearly a million pounds. His time in Spain allowed Barca to break Real Madrid's domination of La Liga and he lifted the league title in his first season. By performing consistently at the highest level domestically he was a shoe-in for the national team and the Dutch were favourites for the 1974 World Cup in Germany. The other teams couldn't cope with their pace and passing and they

demolished everyone to meet the hosts in the final.

The match was billed as a contest between the German efficiency of Franz Beckenbauer and the precocious ability of Cruijff's Dutch. The Dutch scored before the Germans had touched the ball but they couldn't finish the Germans off and Beckenbauer began to dominate the midfield. The home side went on to win 2-1. Cruijff scored five goals and was inspirational in helping his side to the 1976 European Championships in Yugoslavia but the tournament was disappointing and he retired before the 1978 World Cup Finals in Argentina.

He then made a much-publicised move to the North American Soccer League but, despite the big names involved (Pele, George Best, Bobby Moore), the project failed. He returned to Europe to see out his club career and hung up his boots in 1984. He soon took over as manager of Ajax and led them to the KNVB Beker trophy. He also won the European Cup Winners' Cup in 1987. Having moved to Barcelona, he guided the Catalan giants to four consecutive league titles, the Spanish Cup, the Cup Winners' Cup, and the Champions Cup.

He set up the Johan Cruijff Foundation in 1997, which helps improve the lives of under-privileged children.

Thierry Henry

Having had a disappointing 1998/9 season at Juventus, Henry moved to Arsenal and swapped his usual wing position for striker. It proved to be a shrewd buy and an inspired tactical move as Henry, a man blessed with exceptional skill, devastating pace and a fierce shot, soon became the most feared front man in the Premier League. He was also a top-class finisher for France, helping them to the 1998 World Cup and the European Championship trophy in 2000.

Thierry Daniel Henry was born in Paris in 1977. Having not shown much interest in the sport, his father persuaded him to take it more seriously and he showed early promise as a schoolboy while playing for local club side CO Les Ulis. He was then snapped up by AS Monaco as a thirteen-year-old after scoring all six goals in a lower league match. The club insisted he complete an academic course before manager Arsène Wenger gave him his debut, which he subsequently made on the wing in 1994.

Monaco won the 1996/7 league title and, the following year, Henry scored seven goals on their way to the Champions League semi-final. Despite not being completely happy on the wing, he was handed his international debut before the 1998 World Cup and he was an integral part of the side that dominated the tournament. A big-money move to Italian giants Juventus did not go according to plan so Henry followed Wenger to Arsenal.

It was in North London that Henry finally realised his potential. Despite a slow start – he took his time developing into a striker – he helped Arsenal to second place in the league and the final of the 1999 UEFA Cup. On the international front, Henry was the focal point of a team that destroyed the competition and took the European Championship. Domestically, Arsenal finally delivered the success he craved in 2001/2 when they secured the league and cup double but France were the surprise casualties from their group in the 2002 World Cup.

Henry's club form didn't suffer from the ignominy of the early exit and he came second in the 2003 World Player of the Year poll. He delivered again the following season and, along with the likes of Dennis Bergkamp and Patrick Vieira, he helped the Gunners go unbeaten throughout the entire league season, the first time this had been achieved in more than a hundred years.

He broke more records in 2006 when he surpassed Ian Wright and Cliff Bastin's goal-scoring milestones, although Arsenal couldn't edge past Barcelona in the Champions League final. Henry played well at the World Cup in Germany but couldn't help his side overcome Italy in the final. On the domestic front, he joined the Catalans after the tournament and soon helped them to the Copa del Rey, the league title and the Champions League for a unique treble. Having returned from the disastrous World Cup in South Africa, where his team-mates went on strike and refused to train after Nicolas Anelka was sent home, Henry announced his international

retirement and was sold to the New York Red Bulls.

David Beckham

The David Beckham brand is known the world over and is not confined to football. His face is recognised by millions, his life dissected by the frantic media, but, despite all the attention, he remains the consummate football professional. His time in the sport has included the lows of red cards in high-profile matches and the highs of single-handedly dragging the national team to the 2002 World Cup in the Far East.

David Robert Joseph Beckham was born in Leytonstone in May 1975. Unusually for a boy growing up in East London, he became obsessed with Manchester United and aged twelve he enrolled at one of Bobby Charlton's youth football schools in the city alongside future internationals Ryan Giggs, Paul Scholes, Gary Neville, Nicky Butt, Keith Gillespie and Robbie Savage. In 1992 he made his first-team debut against Brighton & Hove Albion in the League Cup before being loaned to Preston North End. He then returned to United and made his league debut against Leeds in 1994/5.

With Beckham playing an increasingly important midfield role, United won the Premier League and the FA Cup double in 1996. Later that year he made his international debut against Moldova in a World Cup qualifier. The following year United defended the league title and Beckham was awarded the PFA Young Player of the Year.

His stock increased further when it emerged that he was dating Victoria Adams of the Spice Girls, but he was left on the bench for England's opening matches at the 1998 World Cup. Beckham then became a national hero when he scored against Colombia and secured their progress to the knockout stages, but hero turned villain when he was sent off against Argentina for deliberately kicking

Diego Simeone. England lost on penalties and Beckham became public enemy number one.

Sir Alex Ferguson managed to get the best out of him on the domestic front and he was instrumental in helping United secure the elusive treble in 1999: the English Premier League; the FA Cup; and, in an epic final, the European Champions Cup against Bayern Munich in Barcelona.

On the international front, however, the public were yet to forgive him and the 2000 European Championships were a disaster. His redemption came first in Munich – where England thrashed Germany 5-1 – and then at Old Trafford when, as captain of his country, he secured England's place at the following World Cup with the finest individual performance of his career, his last-minute free-kick sending a nation delirious, although England lost to eventual winners Brazil in the quarter-final.

After a poor start to the 2003 season, United regained the league title but, after three hundred and ninety-four appearances and eighty-five goals, Real Madrid signed Beckham for twenty-five million pounds. The fans took to him but the team didn't capture a major trophy. Euro 2004 in Portugal was another disappointment for Beckham. His penalty was saved in England's 2-1 defeat by France and the side then lost a shoot-out in the quarter-final to hosts Portugal.

England's confidence before the 2006 World Cup in Germany was also misplaced and the side was knocked out on penalties. Beckham stepped down as captain and new manager Steve McClaren then dropped him from the squad, as did domestic manager Fabio Capello at Real Madrid. So, in January 2007, Beckham signed a five-year contract with Los Angeles Galaxy. His international career looked to be over but he became England's third most capped player in a 2010 World Cup qualifier against Belarus when he earned his 107th cap. He is still hoping to be recalled to the national squad for the 2012 European Championships and the London Olympics.

Beckham has now established several football academies in East London and Los Angeles, and he helped promote London's successful 2012 Olympic bid, as well as becoming a Goodwill Ambassador for the United Nation's Children Fund (UNICEF).

Dino Zoff

A cool and confident goalkeeper of exceptional ability, Dino Zoff was a colossus between the sticks for Juventus and Italy in the 1970s and early '80s. He is the oldest winner of the World Cup, which he lifted as Italy's captain after Spain '82.

Zoff was born in February 1942 in the provincial town of Mariano del Friuli in northern Italy. Despite his goalkeeping aspirations, he was rejected by Inter Milan and Juventus for being too short and thin so he trained as a mechanic while playing for Marianese. He was soon spotted by an Udinese scout but he only made a few appearances before moving to Mantova in 1963. He quickly established himself as a reliable shot-stopper in the first team and after ninety-three appearances he moved to Napoli.

He made his international debut in the qualifying matches for 1968 European Championship against Bulgaria. His side then won the trophy on home soil after beating the Soviet Union in the semi-final (on the toss of a coin after the match ended 0-0) and Yugoslavia after a replayed final. He went on to play a record hundred and twelve times for his country. He also kept a record twelve consecutive clean sheets in a period when the national team began to show its potential. Italy finished fourth at both the 1978 World Cup and 1980 European Championships. Then, at the age of forty, his side finally took the sport's greatest prize, beating giants Argentina, Brazil and West Germany on the way to the World Cup in 1982.

On the domestic front, Zoff is most often associated with Juventus, a club he joined in 1972. His eleven seasons with the Old Lady of Italian football brought him the league six times, the Italian Cup twice and the UEFA Cup in 1977. Zoff retired in 1983 and turned to coaching but, despite victories in the UEFA Cup and the

Coppa Italia, he was sacked in 1990. He then spent four years at Lazio where he became club president, a position he held until being approached to manage the national team in 1998 (he guided them to the runners-up spot at Euro 2000, a match they would have won had France's David Trezeguet not scored a Golden-Goal extra-time winner).

Zoff resigned and returned to Lazio, helping them to third place and qualification for the Champions League in 2000. He then had a brief spell at Fiorentina before stepping down from football at the highest level.

Eusébio

Nicknamed the Black Pearl, Mozambique-born Eusébio became a legendary player for Benfica and Portugal in the 1960s. The striker was quick and possessed a fierce right-foot shot. He made a name for himself on the world stage during the 1966 World Cup in England when he single-handedly guided his side to the semi-final after superb performances against Brazil and South Korea.

Eusébio de Silva Ferreira was born in January 1942 in a poor district of the capital of Mozambique, then a Portuguese colony. He was an excellent young sportsman and began his football career with Sporting Clube de Lorenço Marques. He was soon spotted by Brazilian coach, Bauer, but Brazilian club sides weren't interested and it wasn't until Benfica's coach Bela Guttman saw him play that he was signed.

Eusébio blossomed into a fine footballer at Benfica and he scored twice in the 1962 European Champions Cup final as his team beat the all-conquering Real Madrid side of Ferenc Puskás and Alfredo di Séfano. His prolific goal-scoring record over the following four seasons earned him his first European Footballer of the Year title in 1965. Benfica went on to dominate their domestic league, winning it eleven times, as well as the Portuguese Cup five times.

Eusébio made his international debut for Portugal in a World Cup qualifying match against Luxemburg, which they lost despite being heavy favourites. By 1966, however, Eusébio's Portugal were a more potent force and they beat Hungary 3-1, and then demolished Bulgaria. Then they eliminated Brazil, champions in 1958 and 1962, with Eusébio scoring twice. South Korea surprised them in the quarter-final by taking a 3-0 lead but Eusébio rescued Portugal with four of his country's five goals. He scored again against England in the semi-final but they eventually lost 2-1. Sadly for fans of this little genius, this would be the only international tournament in which he would play.

He retired from top-flight domestic football in 1974 after a bad knee injury, but that didn't stop him heading for the North American League before finally calling it a day in 1978. Eusébio is still recognised today as one of the game's all-time greats alongside Pelé, Maradona and Cruijff.

Gerd Müller

Short but powerfully built, Gerd Müller had a predatory instinct in front of goal and he developed into a scoring machine for club and country. An oft-repeated quote sums up his outstanding ability to score from the most unlikely situations: "He can score standing up, lying down, sitting down and even when falling over. He scores with his head, with his right and left foot, with the knee, his heel and with his toes. Müller even strikes with his stomach and backside."

Gerhard Müller was born in Bavaria in November 1945 and he began playing football with local side TSV 1861 Nördlingen in 1963. He started as he meant to continue, scoring forty-six goals in only thirty-one games, and Bayern Munich soon snapped him up. Although they were in a lower league, Müller's goals helped them to promotion. The following season they finished third in the top flight, won the German Cup and qualified for the European Cup Winners' Cup. They then won the Bundesliga and German Cup double in the 1968 season, with Müller contributing thirty-one goals in thirty games.

Bayern won the league and cup double again in 1972, 1973 and 1974 and they also began to dominate in Europe, winning the European Champions Cup in 1974, 1975 and 1976, a year in which they also won the Intercontinental Cup. His domestic tally of three hundred and sixty-five goals in four hundred and twenty-seven league appearances, eighty goals in sixty-four German Cup games, and sixty-six goals in seventy-four European appearances are records that are likely to stand for some time yet.

He made his international debut against Turkey in 1966 and mirrored his domestic success in the West German team. He eventually scored sixty-eight goals in sixty-two internationals, with Der Bomber peaking during the 1970 World Cup in Mexico. He scored the winner against Morocco, hat-tricks against Bulgaria and Peru, an extra time winner against England in the quarter-final, and two goals in the semi-final against Italy, although in the latter match his heroics were in a losing cause.

His goals finally brought the national team some silverware at the 1972 European Championships in Belgium. Müller scored twice in the semi-final and the final as Germany defeated Belgium and Russia respectively. He retired from international football after sealing victory against the Dutch in the 1974 World Cup. Müller's record tally of fourteen World Cup goals was only beaten by Ronaldo in 2006.

As with so many other stars of the 1970s, Müller moved to America for a couple of seasons and added forty more goals in eighty matches. Life after such a glittering career in football was not as easy as he'd hoped but he recovered from alcoholism to become youth and amateur coach at Bayern Munich. In 2006 he was Munich's ambassador during the 2006 World Cup.

Michel Platini

A gifted attacking midfield playmaker with superb technical ability, Frenchman Michel Platini was so comfortable on the ball that he seemed to be head and shoulders above everyone else on the pitch. He was deadly in front of goal for club and country in the 1980s and now works for UEFA in an official capacity.

Michel François Platini was born in June 1955 in Joeuf in Lorraine, France. Unlike his contemporaries who played professionally having been to the sporting academies, Platini learned to play with his friends in the street. His father started coaching him and reminded him that moving the ball quickly with accurate passing rather than running with it and losing control was the way to keep possession.

While playing for youth side AS Joeuf, he attracted interest from FC Metz but he was injured during his trial and then failed a fitness test. Despite a poor prognosis from the club doctor, he joined AS Nancy-Lorraine in 1972. As he was establishing himself in the squad, he broke his arm, was unable to play and Nancy were relegated, but he scored vital goals the following season and they were promoted as champions.

Platini made his international debut against Czechoslovakia in 1976 and was then selected for the French Olympic team. He was also named in the 1978 World Cup squad but France couldn't progress from a tough group. Despite losing to England in the opening game at the 1982 World Cup, the French then beat Kuwait, Austria and Northern Ireland before they eventually lost to the brutal but brilliant Germans in the semi-final. Platini's best tournament would be the 1984 European Championships on his home turf, however. With Alain Giresse, Luis Fernández and Jean Tigana, Platini completed the carré magique (or magic square), the elegant midfield formation at the heart of the team. Platini was unstoppable, scoring nine of his country's fourteen goals in their five matches, which included the winner in the semi-final and the opener in the final against Spain.

On the domestic front, Platini moved to AS Saint-Étienne when his Nancy contract expired in 1979. He enjoyed moderate success for three years before moving to Juventus where he won numerous honours: the Italian Cup in 1983, the Scudetto in 1984 and 1986, the European Cup Winners' Cup and Super Cup in 1984, the European Champions Cup and Intercontinental Cup in 1985, and the European Footballer of the Year trophy three times, in 1983, 1984, and 1985 (when he was top scorer in the Italian league).

Platini was carrying a groin injury and needed injections to play at the World Cup in Mexico (1986) but he scored vital goals against Italy and Brazil, although the French lost again to West Germany in the semi-final. It was no coincidence that Platini's international retirement brought about a decline in fortunes for the French national team and they failed to qualify for Euro '88 or the 1990 World Cup.

As coach of the national team, he couldn't replicate his former success and he resigned after a poor showing at Euro '92 in Sweden. Today he is President of UEFA, a position he has held since 2006.

Marco van Basten

If he hadn't succumbed to injury during his prime, Marco van Basten would now be talked of as one of the game's true legends. Indeed, he was still one of the most feared strikers in history. He was agile, strong, good in the air, possessed flawless technique and was tactically astute, and he always raised his game for the big occasion. He was one of a rare breed who also enjoyed success as a manager.

Marcel van Basten was born in October 1964 in Utrecht. Aged seven, he began his football career with local club UVV, although his parents believed he would become a gymnast. Ten years later he joined Elinkwijk and his potential was soon spotted by scouts from Ajax, a club he joined in 1981. His debut was as a substitute for Johan Cruijff and he promptly scored his first senior goal. His rise continued unabated and he was the league's top scorer between 1984 and 1987, figures that saw him picked for the national team.

The 1988 European Football Championships in West Germany

saw Van Basten at his best. He scored a hat-trick against England, the winner against the hosts in the semi-final, and an unforgettable volley to sink the Soviet Union in the final. His performances gained him worldwide attention and he was lured to Italian giants AC Milan, and, although the side won the Serie A title, his first season was marred by recurring ankle injuries. The following season, he was fully fit, scored thirty-two goals, and guided the side to European Cup victory over Steaua Bucharest. They defended the trophy the following year against Benfica.

Van Basten had a poor World Cup in 1990 and his form also slipped domestically after arguments with manager Arrigo Sacchi. In 1992, Fabio Capello took over at AC and a revitalised Van Basten helped the club to the title in an unbeaten season. His upsurge in form carried over to the Dutch national team and they reached the semi-final of Euro '92 in Sweden but the tournament's surprise package, Denmark, knocked them out on penalties.

The following season, he was named FIFA and World Soccer Magazine's Player of the Year but the old ankle injury returned and curtailed a brilliant career. His last appearance came in AC Milan's Champions League final defeat by Olympique de Marseille. Having claimed to be retiring from all forms of football, he surprised many by being lured into management and in 2003 he became assistant manager for the Ajax second team. In another controversial move, he was then named as the manager of the Dutch national team the following year.

Van Basten shook up an under-achieving squad and took them to the knockout stages of the 2006 World Cup in Germany where they eventually lost to Portugal, his first competitive defeat as manager. He promptly resigned and took over at Ajax, although he now works as a television pundit.

Peter Schmeichel

The Great Dane is considered the finest goalkeeper of the last twenty years and is ranked by many top professionals as the best in the game. Despite only receiving a wildcard to enter the 1992 European Championships in Sweden, he led Denmark to the title, beating the mighty Germans (then world champions) in the final. Having moved to Manchester United, he was the driving force behind a defence that kept out all-comers and allowed the side to complete a remarkable treble (League Championship, FA Cup and European Championship) in 1999.

Peter Schmeichel was born in Gladsaxe, Denmark, in November 1963. He played his first match just before his ninth birthday and was soon approached by the Gladsaxe Hero youth team coach. He graduated to the senior squad in his late teens and met mentor Svend Hansen. The coach played him in a big match straight away and Schmeichel's performance was praised by the local press.

Hansen then helped him map out his career and he joined Hvidovre in 1985. His side was relegated but Schmeichel had been spotted by Brondby's scouting team and he was signed in 1987. The team won the Danish league in his first season and Schmeichel was soon called up for Denmark. He impressed from the start and was promoted to number one in time for the 1988 European Championships, although the national team couldn't build on his solid performances.

Domestically, Brondby were unstoppable, winning four league titles and reaching the semi-final of the UEFA Cup. It was only a matter of time before the giants of Europe came looking for a superstar goalkeeper and he was bought by Manchester United for half a million pounds, a price that turned out to be the bargain of the century. United were runners-up in his first season but they won the League Cup for the first time in the club's history.

By now Schmeichel was becoming the dominant goalkeeping force on the continent. At the 1992 European Championships in Sweden, the Danes battled through to a semi-final spot against the much-fancied holders, the Netherlands. The match went to penalties and Schmeichel made the decisive save from Marco van Basten. Denmark were criticised for their negative tactics in a dour final against Germany but they scored twice and Schmeichel kept them in the match with marvellous saves from Jürgen Klinsmann, Thomas Häßler and Stefan Effenberg.

He spent the best years of his club career at Manchester United and the side won five Premier League titles, three FA Cups, a League Cup, and the Champions League against Bayern Munich in Barcelona. He then moved briefly to Sporting Lisbon in Portugal before returned to the Premier League with Aston Villa and Manchester City. Having retired, he worked for the BBC and Danish television.

Allying his fearsome reputation with superb technique and determination, Schmeichel pulled off the spectacular and the regulation with consummate ease and he set the standard by which all modern goalkeepers are measured.

Zinedine Zidane

The finest footballer of his generation, Zidane guided an underperforming French team to the World Cup final in 1998, the European Championship in 2000 and a second World Cup final in 2006. Despite his exit for head-butting Marco Matterazzi in the final, he was voted the tournament's best player.

Zidane was born in Marseille in June 1972 to Algerian parents. He grew up in a small apartment in the city and learned to play football in the Place Tartane, which doubled as the block's plaza. When he was ten he joined local side US Saint-Henri before graduating to the French Football Academy. A scout from Cannes spotted him and he made his professional debut in 1989 against Nantes. He had to wait two years for his first goal, which came against the same club, and he remained with Cannes until he was eighteen before signing for Bordeaux. He enjoyed moderate success and helped them to the Intertoto Cup in 1995 but a three-million-pound move to European Champions Juventus soon followed. The

Italians won back-to-back domestic championships but lost out in two European Cup finals. He was banned for head-butting Hamburg's Jochen Kientz but was still voted the best foreign player in Serie A.

International success soon followed. Zidane made his debut against the Czech Republic in 1994 and scored both his country's goals. They were knocked out on penalties by the Czechs in the 1996 European Championships but the side was developing nicely and was expected to do well on home soil at the 1998 World Cup. In a recurring theme, the tournament was characterised by brilliance and stupidity from the mercurial playmaker: France won all of their group matches but he was sent off against Saudi Arabia for stamping on an opponent. He was suspended for the next match but then helped the French beat Italy and Croatia to land a place in the final against Brazil. Zidane scored twice and Emmanuel Petit sealed their emphatic win. Zidane was outstanding in the European Championships two years later and was again named player of the tournament.

He became the world's most expensive footballer when he was bought by Real Madrid for fifty million pounds in 2001. Real won the 2002 Champions League final and La Liga in 2002/03, and Zidane was voted World Player of the Year for the third time. He also collected the award for being the finest European player of the previous half century.

A strong French team with many of the players that had won the previous two major tournaments was expected to perform at the World Cup in 2002 but they played terribly and were dumped out in the group stage having failed to score a single goal. They were below par again at the European Championships in 2004 and were knocked out by Greece, after which Zidane announced his retirement from the national side. He was persuaded to rethink his decision when a number of key players failed to make the 2006 World Cup squad. Zidane promptly guided them to the final with convincing displays against Spain, Brazil and Portugal.

He was presented with the Golden Ball before the final against Italy and duly opened the scoring with a penalty, but Italy equalised and the game went to extra time. With only ten minutes left, Zidane head-butted Marco Matterazzi and was sent off. It was a sad end to a glittering career spanning seventeen years as France then lost the penalty shootout. He is now a special advisor to the Real Madrid team.

Made in the USA
Charleston, SC
14 November 2013